Celebrating Easter and Spring

CELEBRATING EASTER AND SPRING

Compiled by Carl Seaburg and Mark Harris

Original Illustrations by Thomas Dahill

The Anne Miniver Press

Cambridge, Massachusetts: 2000

Printed in the United States of America
Published by the Anne Miniver Press,
P.O. Box 381364, Cambridge, MA 02238-1364
Text design by Joan Tuttle

ISBN#0-9720896-0-8

To Andrea, my continuing source of new life

"Each day the world is born anew"
James Russell Lowell

Contents

Preface

The traditional Christian church year is divided into three seasons: ADVENT, the coming of Jesus; LENT, the death of Jesus; and PENTECOST, the early history of the Christian church.

In Unitarian Universalist congregations, the first two seasons are usually celebrated, the third is not. The anthology "Celebrating Christmas" provides helpful material for UU congregations to honor ADVENT. This anthology, "Celebrating Easter and Spring," provides similar material to honor LENT.

Two other helpful anthologies in this series are "Great Occasions" which contains material for celebrating the important passages of an individual's life: birth, coming of age, marriage, and death; and "The Communion Book" which provides some 66 communion services used in UU congregations to honor the ties that bind us together.

The materials in this collection are all from Unitarian Universalist sources. We are greatly indebted to all who have contributed to this anthology, particularly those who shared their files with us. Special thanks go to the work of Barbara Hutchins and Jacqui James. The selections are broadly diverse to meet the many tastes and viewpoints within the denomination.

Some hold that Easter is an uneasy celebration for Unitarian Universalists. We would argue the opposite. Easter is part of our human heritage. We may not believe in the physical resurrection of Jesus, but we can see in that celebration the message of renewal.

Mostly the older pieces have been made gender inclusive. In a very few cases we have left some historic items as originally written for their antique flavor. But you will find that you can easily adapt them to current language use.

We have tried to give proper credit to all the authors of the pieces included. In case of error, we apologize and will make corrections in future editions if we are so informed. The illustrations in this book are suitable for use as Sunday service covers so feel free to reproduce them.

Carl Seaburg
Mark W. Harris

This manuscript was nearly completed when Carl died in December 1998. I cannot sum up what Carl contributed to our movement as historian, raconteur, bibliophile, and immense contributor to our worship life with his published anthologies, along with historical writings and hymn texts. Most of all, Carl was a wonderful person, a sweetheart of a guy. We will all miss him.

M.W. H.

Sponsors

When I have fears that I may cease to be
Before my pen has glean'd my teeming brain,
Before high-piled books, in charactery,
Hold like rich garners the full ripen'd grain

John Keats

About a year before Carl Seaburg died, he read this poem at a small dinner party in London; half way through he broke down in tears and was unable to finish.

These individuals and congregations listed below – through their financial support – have made the "full ripen'd grain" of his and Mark Harris's efforts – along with the creative work of their Unitarian Universalist colleagues – possible. Truly, no pen need ever cease to be.

Nancy Light
Carolyn and Robert Bell
Ann, William, Elizabeth, and Sarah
   Thomas
David Light and Rose Granado
Alison, Robert, Alexander, Henry,
   and Ian Light
Maria, Thomas, Sonia, Samantha
   and Thomas Carl Hittle
Maria Grossman
Woody and Trudi Widrick
Eugene McAfee
Kathy Duhon
Kenneth W. Sawyer
Cynthia A. Foster
Martha and David Pohl
John Hurley
Janet Bowering
Dorothy and Herbert Vetter
Priscilla Murdock
Barbara and William DeWolfe
Linda S. Yeaton

Pat Bowen
John Gibbons
Freda Carnes
In memory of Jean Newhall Seaburg
   and Agnes E. Peterson
The Congregation of the Unitarian
   Universalist Church of Medford,
   Massachusetts
The Congregation and Calvin O.
   Dame of the Unitarian Universalist
   Community Church, Augusta,
   Maine
The Congregation of the First Parish
   of Concord, Massachusetts
The Congregation of The First Parish
   Church, Unitarian Universalist,
   Saugus, Massachusetts
The Congregation of The First Parish
   of Watertown, Massachusetts
The Congregation of The First
   Universalist Church, Norway,
   Maine

I. The Call of Easter

O Life that maketh all things new,
The blooming earth, our thoughts within.
Our pilgrim feet, wet with thy dew,
In gladness hither turn again.

Samuel Longfellow

A Short History of Easter and Spring

Carl Seaburg

In the Christian calendar Easter is a moveable feast. Christmas is always December 25, but Easter can vary by more than a month. It can never be earlier than March 22, nor later than April 25. The date was fixed in 325 C.E. by the Council of Nicea and was set as the Sunday after the first full moon after or on the Spring equinox. In the Christian community it is celebrated as the great feast of the resurrection of Jesus.*

Spring has a set calendar date. Theoretically it begins on the Spring equinox, which is always March 21. But the weather doesn't pay attention to our calendars, so we can have snowstorms on the "official" date of Spring. Spring comes when the weather gets around to it. And in the Southern hemisphere it comes in our Northern fall. So Spring is a moveable feast, too.

Over the centuries the Christian church has kept adding to the Easter celebration. The countdown to Easter in a traditional Christian church now begins after Mardi Gras ("Fat Tuesday") on what is called Ash Wednesday, the beginning of Lent.

In England Shrovetide is the name for the last 3 or 4 days before the beginning of Lent, including Egg Saturday, Quinquagesima Sunday, Collop Monday, and Shrove Tuesday.

This was a season of high carnival in many European countries. In earlier times the Lenten fast was more rigorous than it is now, so the carnival was celebrated by wild revelries, games, sports, dances, and riotous antics. Food that couldn't be eaten during the fast was eaten during this period.

Shrove Tuesday—known as Mardi Gras in the United States—marks the splendid climax of the carnival with parades and outrageous costumes, revelry and inevitable pranks and mischief. A season of freedom from ordinary rules was permitted, full of noisy fun and masquerades, practical jokes and ridicule.

Ash Wednesday began to be celebrated from about 1250 C.E. Its name came from the ceremonial use of ashes to mark the forehead of believers as a symbol of penitence. The ashes came from the burning of palms that had been consecrated on Palm Sunday the previous year. It was an outgrowth of the custom of public penance in the early days of the church.

Lent, a word from Old English that meant spring, marked a period of fasting and penitence in preparation for the celebration of Easter. It lasted forty week-days until Easter. In England for many years, the fourth Sunday in Lent was known as Mothering Sunday, when children brought small cakes called simnel as a present to their mothers. The cake is described as looking like a pork pie, but was a rich plum pudding.

Palm Sunday is the beginning of the Easter week activities and was observed before 1000 c.e. It marked the ceremonial entry of Jesus into Jerusalem where he had come to celebrate the Passover.

Customarily it is celebrated with palm branches and the distribution of palm crosses in churches. The association of palms or willows with this Sunday of early spring is a common custom. In England the sallow willow with its large and beautiful catkins often takes the place of the palm. People often decorate their houses with them or wear them as sprigs in their hats. The feeling was that it brought good luck and protected the house from harm.

The Passover is a spring festival celebrated by the Jews. Originally it is said to have been a agricultural observance marking the birth of the lambs and dating from the desert period. Later it was broadened to commemorate the exodus of the Jews from Egypt.

The Thursday before Easter is known as Maundy Thursday. The name came from the Latin words, "novum mandatum," of Jesus' words to the disciples after he had washed their feet. Since he has washed his disciples feet, this was the chief ceremony to mark his last supper with them. It was not practiced in the early church but has been kept since the middle ages with bishops and the pope wash-ing the feet of 12 poor men or beggars. Queen Elizabeth is said to have per-formed the ceremony while James II was the last English monarch to do so. Today in most Protestant churches it is an occasion to hold a communion ser-vice. Many UU congregations celebrate this communion by commemorating all those members of the congregation who have died in the previous year. Some note both the "Last Supper" and Passover. Maundy Thursday is said to get its name from the Latin word mandatum, meaning a command. And is in reference to the new commandment Jesus gave at the last supper.

The next day was called Good Friday, an odd name to mark the day Jesus was crucified, but it is thought to be a corruption of "God's Friday," its original name. In some countries it is known as Long Friday. In Roman Catholic churches the altar is draped in black, and this custom has been picked up by some Protestant churches. Frequently a three hour service is held from noon until 3 p.m. which is the time Jesus is thought to have died. The service is marked by prayers and sermons on what are called "the seven last words of Jesus."

Then Easter Sunday itself arrives. The churches are joyfully decorated, filled with flowers and greenery, and in some the great Paschal candle is lit and burns from thence onward to Ascension Day. The lily has come to be regarded as the supreme Easter flower.

English hot cross buns are frequently eaten for breakfast. The shiny brown tops of the buns are marked with a frosting cross. It is customary to wear new clothes at Easter—at least a new hat. But long before Easter people put on fresh new garments at the Spring Festival, it signaled joy for the winter that was past. Many families serve colored Easter eggs as part of the breakfast fare. And the youngsters have fun trying to bang their eggs against each others to see which one will outlast the others. A traditional Easter dinner is often lamb with mint sauce, though now an Easter ham frequently takes the place of the lamb.

The day often begins by churches holding Easter sunrise services outdoors. This developed from an old belief that the sun danced at its rising on Easter morning for joy that Jesus had risen from the grave. You had to be up early to witness it.

Easter Monday used to be a day for games and sports and merriment in England, but like many other old customs this has died away in the United States. Today Easter ends on Easter, but in olden times Easter festivities continued through Hocktide, the name given to the Monday and Tuesday after Low Sunday.

Forty days after Easter comes Ascension Sunday. Then, nine days later on Whitsun Eve, Easter formally ends and the third great cycle of the church year begins and continues to Advent.

In every country that Christianity invaded, it found that the inhabitants already were holding festivals and rituals marking the spring season. Many of the local customs in time were grafted on to the Christian celebration. In England, for example, the celebration of Fig Sunday and the ritual of blessing the wells, are remnants of the older festivals. One could say that our Easter was married to the older Spring celebrations. Or put another way, that our Easter celebrations highjacked the earlier Spring rituals.

It was only natural that early people should notice and mark in a ceremonial fashion, the time of year when nature seemed to revive after the rest of winter—those who kept sheep found that lambs were born then; those responsible for crops knew that was the time to plant and renew them. Everything around them testified to the renewal of life as birds returned and trees leaved out and wild flowers grew again.

So it was only natural, too, that people developed rituals to ensure abundant crops and to use magic to ward off disasters such as droughts and bad harvests. Incorporated into those celebrations were the fertility rites of their own personal lives. Ancient people made use of sexual symbolism to encourage the fertility of their herds and fields. The early Christians stamped out such mating rituals wherever they found them. Some might find this an improvement. Others of us find it a loss.

---

* Setting the date for Easter was not without controversy. In 664 a synod of the English church met at Whitby to determine whether they would follow the Roman or Celtic method for dating Easter. The Roman method prevailed after King Oswy of Northumbria determined that he did not want to alienate St. Peter, who he feared might turn his back on those waiting to enter the gates of heaven. Easter falls differently for orthodox Christianity which, unlike western Christianity, did not accept the Gregorian calendar reform in 1582. Orthodox Christians celebrate Easter on the Sunday following Passover.

Will There Always Be an Easter?

Joan Goodwin

Will there always be an Easter? Hundreds of years from now, when people know more and travel farther than we even dream of now. . .

will there be an Easter then?

Yes, as long as there is an Earth planet
and a sun
and springtime
and people who wonder about death and celebrate life . . .
for as long as that, there will be an Easter.

Easter got its name from the direction of the sun's rising. After the longest night of the year, people watched the sun rise in the East a little earlier and a little higher in the sky week by week. In some northern countries, people would climb through the late winter snow to the mountain tops, and on each crest bonfires would blaze up to show the sun the way. Sometimes they tied bunches of straw to huge wheels, set the straw on fire, and rolled the flaming circles along to help the sun return.

Even before calendars, people knew that the longer days meant melting snow, softening soil, growing time, and another harvest of food to keep their families fed . . . another year of life to live.

Once people understood how plants and animals reproduce, once they became gardeners and tenders of flocks, aware of the results of their own lovemaking, they consciously participated, as partners with the gods, in the great life process. Planting time became a victory over death. Symbols of new life were held sacred: the seed, the flower, the egg, the organs of human sexuality, the newborn of all animals, and especially the fertile rabbit.

Ancient Egyptians thought of their rich valley as a woman, the goddess Isis, and of the great Nile River as the god Osiris, flooding the land each year with life-giving water. Their story says that Set, a jealous brother, killed Osiris and scattered his remains along the river bank. Isis lovingly put Osiris together and brought him back to life. After his resurrection, he lived forever as ruler over the souls of the dead in the Elysian Fields. The story was re-enacted in spring celebrations for centuries and must have been known by the Hebrew slaves before the time of Moses.

Babylonians told the story of Tammuz, god of the harvest, who died young, and of Ishtar, goddess of love, who rescued him from the underworld. Phoenicians had a similar story about Adonis and Aphrodite.

The rituals of death and rebirth for these gods were observed by neighbors of the Hebrews who reclaimed their Promised Land, bringing with them another springtime celebration, the Passover. One of the great stories of all time, mixing reality and imagination, told and retold in the camps of a wandering tribe, and finally written down in a patchwork of many versions, Passover tells Jewish people everywhere to this day that their god kept his covenant with his chosen people and overpowered their enemies. Because the Egyptian Pharaoh refused the Hebrew slaves religious freedom, Moses, his brother Aaron, and their god Yahweh brought one affliction after another to the Egyptians. Finally Yahweh passed through the land by night, bringing death to the first-born of every Egyptian family. So that the Hebrews would be spared, he told them to kill a lamb and mark their doorways with its blood. When Yahweh came to a door marked with the blood of the lamb, he would pass over that house.

Generation after generation, the Jews have celebrated this Passover according to instructions given them by Yahweh through Moses. Ancient symbols—the egg, new green leaves, the lamb—were used again, along with unleavened bread and wine, in this freedom festival each spring.

It was a Passover seder meal that Jesus shared with his disciples on that last Thursday of his life. Undoubtedly many of his people hoped that he would set them free from the Romans who then occupied their Promised Land. And it must have been partly fear that he might try to lead an uprising which caused the Romans to seize him and bring him to trial. The Jewish officials were more concerned with another kind of freedom which Jesus preached—freedom from the old laws, freedom to live in a new Promised Land, an open community of humanness and love which he called the Kingdom of God.

So hundreds of years after that original Passover, Jesus was crucified. People said that God had sacrificed his own firstborn son, and they called Jesus "the lamb of God." His followers could not accept his death. Surely if he was the Messiah, the son of god as they suspected, he could rise again and have eternal life, like the old nature gods whose stories they may well have remembered.

Once again the ancient story elements were revived as they told of Mary and the other women going to the tomb of Jesus and meeting the angel who said, "He is risen. Why seek you the living among the dead?"

And a new ritual observance began, followed by generation after generation of Christians, who re-enact in the Mass, the crucifixion and resurrection of Jesus and partake of his strength and spirit with the unleavened bread and the wine of that last seder supper.

Other great leaders have died in the cause of freedom and a larger life for their people . . . leaders like Lincoln, Gandhi, King. We know now, even without elaborate myth-making, that they shall have eternal life as long as we keep their memories green and their lifework growing.

We know that we are all godlike partners in the life process and that we must be careful in our cleverness lest we create some year a silent spring.

We are "children born of Earth's desiring,"

life evolved to self-awareness,

using death for new birth,

generation after generation,

that life may be eternal,

just as it is in the stories we have told from the beginning.

Celebrating Easter: The Many Ways Unitarian Universalists Find Meaning

Mark W. Harris

The resurrection of Jesus Christ from the dead is the central Easter message for Christians, but the idea of celebrating a risen savior makes most religious liberals ignore the concept of resurrection entirely. Historically, our Unitarian Universalist approach has been to talk about Jesus the great ethical teacher. A third way to look at the idea of resurrection neither affirms nor denies its reality, but asks us to celebrate the alternative ways we experience resurrection. A resurrection occurs in the wake of a startling life transformation. What will set us free?

We Unitarian Universalists can celebrate Easter by asking when resurrection is a reality for all of us. If we believe in a creative power which shatters the icy tomb of winter with the life-giving miracle of spring, we have seen a resurrection. If we believe in a creative power which moves tens and then tens of thousands of people to cry out against the injustices of society, enabling the downfall of hatred and prejudice, then we have fomented a resurrection. If we believe in a creative power lying within each human breast which enables us to break the bonds of personal pain and know the hope of new tomorrows, then we have experienced a resurrection.

At Eastertide Unitarian Universalists celebrate the many resurrections of the season. We celebrate the glories of the earth when birds take to the wing and crocuses force their way through the crust of snow to announce the arrival of spring. We celebrate the untold numbers of courageous individuals and groups who have sacrificed their lives to liberate others from oppression and create a more just and loving world. We celebrate the ability of the human heart to overcome personal tragedy or disability and affirm once again the strength to love or excel when many others would have given up all hope. Easter celebrates the times of witnessing, experiencing, and creating the resurrections of human life.

For centuries before the advent of Christianity, human beings celebrated the rebirth of the earth in spring from the cold tomb of winter. In a patterned sequence, an unseen and unknown creative power brought a profound change to their natural habitat. Our prehistoric ancestors' utter dependence upon a fruitful and flowering earth made the coming of this season of renewed growth an important festival of life. "Here comes the sun," was the joyous cry as a warm glow shown brightly upon the world.

We believe the word Easter derives from an Anglo-Saxon goddess of the dawn, Eastre. Her principal festival was celebrated at the vernal equinox. Easter reminds us of the East, where the sun rises, and the power for ongoing life and light originate. In the spring, after months of lifeless cold, each one of us instinctively feels our spirits lift when greater amounts of this life-giving light come into our lives. We watch flowers bend and stretch towards this energy while defying ice and frost. All of our scientific knowledge does not diminish the sense of mystery and devotion we feel towards our beautiful planet. With fears of global warming and other ecological disasters resulting from human destructiveness, the need to celebrate and uphold the great interdependence we have with the world and all its creatures becomes more vital to all Unitarian Universalists. We resurrect with the earth by learning to feel at home with our bodies, while experiencing a sense of oneness with all of creation.

If some Unitarian Universalists celebrate a spring festival, others honor our Judaic roots with the Passover. This celebration recalls the deliverance of the Hebrew people from their slavery in Egypt. This ancient story proclaims humanity's longing for liberty and justice for all. It has proven a mighty inspiration to countless people who suffered under some kind of oppression. Our Puritan ancestors saw themselves as being delivered from religious oppression in England. African-American slaves felt a kinship with Moses and echoed his cry to "Let my people go." Countless generations have been willing to risk their lives for some kind of freedom.

In the spirit of Moses and Aaron and Miriam, liberals celebrate and participate in efforts to broaden the human concept of freedom. We see it as a religious imperative to act on behalf of those who may be enslaved by the hatred, fear, or bigotry of others. Freedom from any form of oppression is a resurrection to a new life of dignity and worth. This is the political understanding of the season, and it is exemplified by any means of working towards achieving greater justice in the world. From the long journey of the Jews towards freedom, to Jesus' feeding the hungry and turning over the money changers' tables, to active participation by any one of us today to stand in solidarity with those who are victims of homophobic hate crimes or the like, Unitarian Universalists mean to speak and act on behalf of anyone who might be victimized by the cruel or heartless actions of others.

Central to many religious liberals' understanding of the Easter season is a fresh look at the life, death, and resurrection of Jesus. Some Unitarian Universalists use this time to rekindle their awareness of our Christian origins, but for many others it is a matter of deep personal faith. An understanding of the meaning of the story of Jesus' resurrection may begin with the disciples and the powerful vision of Jesus that continued to live in their hearts after he died. They began to believe that the impossible could become the possible and that personal strength and renewal could come to them in the context of a new community. Thus, the Church was born.

Part of the Christian story is the pain and fear one person must face in confronting death. A critical part of the Easter message for Unitarian Universalists is the power within each of us to face death, and find a life-giving power even in our most harrowing moments of illness or despair. There is great undying potential buried beneath lifelessness and hopelessness. In the resurrection story there is both humiliation and death, but in the end also a new life of the spirit. For us it means confronting the deep wounds and scars we have suffered and then allowing ourselves to be transformed anew.

When we are enslaved by bonds of sorrow or hate or greed the experience of turning our lives in a new direction means we can forgive ourselves for imperfections. When this forgiveness occurs we are free to reach out and begin fulfilling lives of genuine human sharing. It is what happens to Scrooge in Charles Dickens' *A Christmas Carol.* Something forces him to look at the pain and misery, and he becomes a changed man. Greed becomes generosity, as he vows to "turn human misery into joy." When any one of us survives and "comes back" from a life-changing event such as an illness or accident, we often feel a tremendous sense of gratitude for life. Then in response to our appreciation for being given time to continue living and loving, we become a new person.

The Easter or Spring season can provide additional meanings for Unitarian Universalists through such resurrection themes as the human hope for life after death, or at least a sense that life is "deathless," and continues in new forms. Others might see an affirmation of the human body with the resurrection story portraying the importance of the body when Jesus emphasizes touching him when he appears before the disciples during a shared meal.

The central message of the resurrection for many religious liberals though is the human potential to overcome serious personal loss or failure and begin to live a more whole life. When we think of our earth's ability to regenerate itself, our political ability to join forces with others to overcome the human predilection for violently excluding others, and finally, our personal ability to recover from a seemingly empty or forsaken life, then the meaning of the season can become powerful for many Unitarian Universalsits. We can make the "resurrection" a reality in our lives. It is I, you, and they who are risen from the dead. The traditional cry of "he lives" becomes "we live."

(This is a revised version of the UUA pamphlet, Celebrating Easter: Reflections of a Unitarian Universalist.)

II. O Day of Light and Gladness

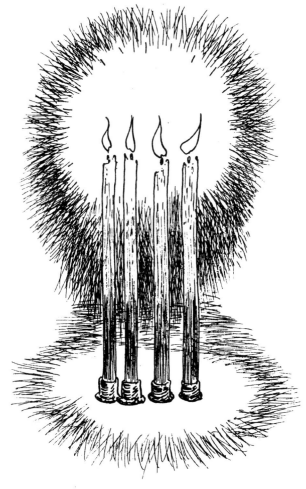

O day of light and gladness,
of prophesy and song,
what thoughts within us waken,
what hallowed mem'ries throng!

Frederick Lucian Hosmer

Opening and Closing Words

Opening Words: Lent

Lent is the tough road to Easter, for Jesus and for us all, the smell of lilac, the cost of tears.

— Clarke Dewey Wells

A Lenten Diet

Fast from criticism, and feast on praise;
Fast from self-pity, and feast on joy;
Fast from ill-temper, and feast on peace;
Fast from resentment, and feast on contentment;
Fast from jealousy, and feast on love;
Fast from pride, and feast on humility;
Fast from selfishness, and feast on service;
Fast from fear, and feast on faith.

— John B. Wolf

Opening Words: Easter

Creator of earth's merry-go-round of times and seasons
    (wheeling day and night—
    birth, growth, fulfillment, descent to rest)
and of the seasons of the human heart,
we would enter into awareness of the inward world shared by our
deepest selves.
Be with us as we welcome, each in our own way, this high season:
    Spring for awakening,
    Passover for freedom,
    Easter for hope against hope—
    all for love.

— Greta W. Crosby

We gather this morning in the face of mystery.
We hear the birdsong, knowing from their triumphal
    entry that the time of winter is over.
We sense the presence around us of life: ongoing, energetic,
    embodied in women and men and children.
Their smiles, their cares, their concerns come before us now.
In the silence of this morning let us give praise for life,
    for all its changes,
    for all its unpredictable caprices,
    for its sustaining graces.
In this silence let us sense the eternal presence of life
    in our veins, in our bodies, in the electrical flash
    from eye to eye as people meet and touch and
    heal each other. Amen.

— Mark Mosher DeWolfe

Sing, O heavens, and be joyful, O earth;
And break forth into singing, O mountains:
For God hath comforted the people.

— Isaiah 49:13

We are here because we are alive, because we would rather be alive
than dead.

*We are here because we have received life as a gift—because
despite all the contradictions we believe the gift is good.*

We have come this day to celebrate life and to say thank you for the gift
of the rain and the sun.

*We have come to share our lives with one another, that our
sorrows may be lightened, our joys doubly gladdened, and the
fullness of life known and proclaimed in all its pain and glory.*

We are thankful for the gift of being together. We are thankful for
being. We are thankful for life.

— Richard M. Fewkes
(adapted from an anonymous source)

Build thee more stately mansions, O my soul,
As the swift seasons roll!
Leave thy low-vaulted past!
Let each new temple, nobler than the last,
Shut thee from heaven with a dome more vast,
Till thou at length art free,
Leaving thine outgrown shell by life's unresting sea!

– Oliver Wendell Holmes

O God of Easter: we gather together this day to celebrate the return of spring after the long hard winter, the resurrection of life after death, and the revival in our hearts of confidence, trust, and hope. Come into our presence during this hour, teaching us to attend to that which springs afresh in our lives, that we may continually be open to the new, the revitalizing, the transforming, which is a very miracle in our midst.

– Dianne Arakawa

For Easter eggs and Easter flowers,
    For Easter song and story,
For Easter gladness in our hearts,—
    To God be praise and glory.

– Vincent Silliman

May this, our coming together for worship and prayer on this Easter Sunday morning, be not simply a duty, but an exalted experience whose influence shall go with us through the coming week. We come here for the uplifting of heart and mind which we receive. More than all else may it be a waiting in the presence of all that is good in the experiences of people everywhere, that our little lives and common concerns may be illumined with the glow of a living faith. May the miracle of springtime, one of the millions that have dawned over the world, keep alive in our hearts the child-like wonder in the presence of the ancient but ever new pageant of nature.

– Alfred S. Cole

The souls of the righteous are in the hand of God,
And no torment shall touch them.
They are at peace,
And their hope is full of immortality.

— Wisdom III: 1,3,4

Today we come—as people have come for thousands of years
   —to worship and sing praises
   —to celebrate the victory of hope over despair
   —to be reminded of the ever renewing life of the spirit
   —and to mark the season of springtime come again.
Hallelujah! Hallelujah!
Welcome to our festival of joy!

— Polly Leland-Mayer

We look not at things which are seen, but at the things which are not seen; for the things which are seen are temporal, but the things which are not seen are eternal.

— II Cor. IV: 18

We welcome Easter morning as a festival of the living body.

May its story remind us never to separate ourselves from our life in the body.

May we feel that body and spirit are one; that flesh is good.

May we be in touch with our hands and feet; every living, breathing part of ourselves.

May we love the body: as regenerating earth, as reproducing seed, as immortal release into the great beyond and back; each one of us the word made flesh.

Praise the body!

— Mark W. Harris

We are here

to link our memory of love past,

and our hope for deeper love to come,

in this present hour of thanksgiving and praise...

Lo, how fly the years! Another Easter is upon us.

Once again, the flowers unfold like our best dreams.

Once again the color and fragrance surprise us, as if for the first time.

Once again life stretches and reaches beyond its own horizon!

Once again the day of sheer Alleluia dawns

and we are glad to be alive to see it.

Praise!

– Mark Belletini

Come with me, this morning, to the uplands and high places of the spirit, that together we may front the vast horizons of life and death. In the clear light of Easter we will gain deeper insights into the wonder and mystery surrounding us. On this journey we will take all people with us for we are the children of Mother Earth. May all the hopes and dreams of the great souls of the race, the song of the bird, and the flush of Spring across the hills, bring us renewed faith and joy.

– Alfred S. Cole

Chalice Lightings: Easter

We give thanks for life reborn.
We give thanks for joy to overcome loss and pain.
We give thanks for the earth as it blooms its renewal.
We give thanks that all living things are revived.
As a sign of our gratitude, we light this chalice to welcome all new
songs of life.

– Mark W. Harris

Glory be to the earth and the wind.
Glory be to the sun and rain.
Glory be to animals and children
    and women and men.
Glory be to our holy flame
    which calls us together as one.

– Bettye A. Doty

Chalice Lightings: Spring

Gathering in our church, we light this chalice as a symbol of our
    thankfulness.
The chalice reminds us of the sun, the giver of life.
The chalice flame rises up like the power of growth and renewal in
    the springtime.
While lighting the chalice we give thanks for the sun, which lights
    and warms the earth
For the growth and renewal of nature, arising from the earth. And for
    the earth itself, which is also the giver of life.

– David J. Miller

Opening Words: Spring

Gathering together this morning from many directions, we give
thanks for the beauty of spring, the warmth of the sun, and the
breadth of the holy spirit that called us to worship.

– Bettye A. Doty

Enough

Birdsong again
a blossoming tree—
Spring is enough
Resurrection for me.

– Dorothy Parsons East

Spring has burst forth with its wet welcome, and now with its
clear skies.

The seasons of our souls respond with gladness that new Life shall
welcome us to another year of growing.

Let us celebrate our meeting here today;

Let us be lifted with the new season;

Let us turn from side to side with eyes that meet and with smiles that
proclaim our community,

We pause together out of the midst of separate lives

to give thanks,

to be strengthened and refreshed,

and to share our search for wisdom and for gentleness.

— Bruce Southworth

Seasons of the Self

We need a celebration that speaks the Spring-inspired word about
life and death,

About us as we live and die,

Through all the cycling seasons, days, and years.

*We need the sense of deity to crack our own hard, brown
December husks.*

And push life out of inner tombs and outer pain.

*Unless we move the seasons of the self, and Spring can come
for us,*

The winter will go on and on.

*And Easter will remain a myth, and life will never come again,
despite the fact of Spring.*

— Max A. Coots

We call forth this morning the spirit of Spring, of Creation, of
Rejuvenation. As the earth slowly awakes from its long sleep so each
of us stirs beneath the slumber of apathy in anticipation of the Great
Mystery of Life.

As buds and bulbs swell with potency so our spirits feel the full weight of their soulful pregnancy and prepare to give birth to our empowering potential.

We call forth the spirit of Spring this morning within each of us, the spirit that moves us to transform who we are into who we can be.

We call forth the life-giving spirit to unveil our love for this creation, to bring healing to those in pain, and to sing the song of the spirit.

– Michael A. McGee

Gratitude

Often I have felt that I must praise my world
For what my eyes have seen these many years,
And what my heart has loved.
And often I have tried to start my lines:
   "Dear earth," I say
   And then I pause
   To look once more.
   Soon I am bemused
   And far away in wonder.
So I never get beyond "Dear Earth."

– Max A. Kapp

From out the glory of the morning skies
The Life Giver calls to us "Arise!
Out of eternity—behold a day!
A gift for you to spend some way.
What will you do with it, I say?"

From out the glory of the setting sun
The Life Giver call, "What have you done
With the day that has gone?
Never more will the day return,
However strongly you may yearn."

Use wisely then this gift to you—
Fresh from God like heaven's dew.
Miracles are waiting in it—
Of beauty, you can create anew—

Of love reborn, of efforts true.
Your heaven may be hiding in it.
Use wisely then life's gift to you.

– Sophia Lyon Fahs

At this season when the cold winds cease and gentle sunshine wakens the earth, when field and garden are clothed in new radiance, we would keep our mind and heart open to the beauty of nature and the splendour of the spirit. As winter yields to spring, so may the coldness of our hearts yield to the gladness of the world, and the new life of earth find response in the renewal of our human lives. Thus shall we become worthy participants in the great life which out of the old eternally brings forth the new.

– *compiled by* Peter B. Godfrey

Greenup

From this rough
bark open tender
leaves. Lively
green leaps out
of the dull brown.

Waiting winterlong,
the buds have burst.

What inner
knowing calls
these leaves and birds
returning to sing
among them?

– Joan Goodwin

For lo, the winter is past
The rain is over and gone
The flowers appear on the earth
The time of the singing of birds is come
And the voice of the turtledove is heard in the land.

– Song of Solomon 2: 11,12

Closing Words: Easter

May you have joy this Easter, a joy born of life well lived;
May you have love this Easter, a love stronger than death,
   bringing healing and new growth to your life,
   and light where it feels dark;
And may you have peace this Easter, peace which allows you
   to be open to the newness of the season,
   and gives you reason to sing.

– Judith G. Mannheim

Like jelly beans and chocolate rabbits, may each season's special
delights always bring you sustaining joy. Like the bunny's hidden
presents in the springtime grass, may surprises and unseen givers ever
lead you to give thanks. Like cheeping newborns from chicken's eggs
and opening crocuses, dewy fresh, may the miracle of life fill you with
awe forevermore. Amen.

– Colleen M. McDonald

Let the horizon of our minds
include all people:
the great family here on earth with us;
those who have gone before
and left us the heritage
of their memory and of their works;
and those who lives will be shaped
by what we do
or leave undone.

– Samuel McChord Crothers

We celebrate the resurrection of the spirit, exemplified in nature
through the miracle of spring, symbolized in the story of Jesus,
manifest in the best of us. As spring laughs today, at long last
victorious over winter, so Jesus must have laughed, when he saw that

even in death, he was taken up in the mystery of life, so may we, in joy and laughter, embrace each other, and embrace life, in all its ambiguity and downright messiness, on this Easter morning.

– Charles S. Slap

Easter is an impossible story written for everyone who has ever felt the sting of death and wishes for something more.

Easter is a story for anyone who loves life so much that they pray for more life to follow.

Easter is a story for people who can envision a loving divinity that will not be conquered by evil.

It's a story of love that never dies;
of immoveable objects that get tossed aside;
of happy endings in a tragic world;
of miracles;
of faith rewarded and vision restored and hope justified.
That's what Easter is.

– Patrick O'Neill

Closing Words: Spring

Green grass sustain us.
Green earth uphold us.
Green peace transform us.
In the name of God,
Allelulia!

– Andrew Hill

May the spirit of life, a gift of the earth's renewal, come awake inside us again. And may we find it holy!

– Judith Meyer

O God, so touch us with the soul's eternal springtime that no wintry hour of life shall blight our faith or freeze our hearts.

– A. Powell Davies

May the warm sun
Shine upon you.

May the brightness of the green grass
Fill you with exultation.

May the sweet perfume of the spring flowers
Scent the place where you stand.

May the songs of the birds
Bring music to your soul.

And love
Fresh and bright
Renew your life.

– Roland E. Morin

The Dance of Life

Teach us to dance, O Life,
Till we find ourselves
"At the still point of the turning world"
And know ourselves to be one with thee and each other,
Brothers and sisters of the One Life
That has died and risen again and again
In the springtime renewal of human consciousness.

– Richard M. Fewkes

III. Wake, Now, My Senses

Wake, now, my senses, and hear the earth call,
Feel the deep power of being in all,
Keep with the web of creation your vow,
Giving, receiving as love shows us how.

Thomas J. S. Mikelson

Poetry: Easter

Prayer for Easter (for A.C.S.)

Lord God of Easter and infrequent Spring,
Thaw our wintry hearts.
Announce the large covenant to deceitful lands,
Drive the sweet liquor through our parched veins.
Stir the vacant eyes with green explosions
        and gold in azure sky.
Smite the pall of death that hangs like desire:
Lure us to fresh schemes of life.
Rouse us from tiredness, self-pity,
Whet us for use;
Fire us with good passion,
Rekindle thy Church.
Restore in us the love of living,
Bind us to fear and hope again.
      As we thank with brief thanksgiving,
      Whatever odds may be,
      That life goes on living,
      That the dead rise up ever,
      That even the weariest river
      Winds back to springs under the sea.

                       – Clarke Dewey Wells

Easter Morn

On eyes that watch through sorrow's night,
   On aching hearts and worn,
Rise thou with healing in thy light,
   O happy Eastern Morn!

The dead earth wakes beneath thy rays,
   The tender grasses spring;
The woods put on their robes of praise,

And flowers are blossoming.

O shine within the spirit's skies,
  Till, in thy kindling glow,
From out the buried memories
  Immortal hopes shall grow.

Till from the seed oft sown in grief,
  And wet with bitter tears,
Our faith shall bind the harvest sheaf
  Of the eternal years!

– Frederick Lucian Hosmer (1890)

Easter: I hope he'll be remembered

I hope he'll be remembered—
Obscured by centuries of violence,
Clouded by countless creeds,
Dissected by a thousand scholars,
Preached from a million pulpits,
Mouthed by a million lips,
Crucified by willful distortion
And innocent ignorance.
I hope he'll be remembered
In simple, unadorned humanity.

– Richard S. Gilbert

On Immortality

We are not isolated from nature.
We are not isolated in our thinking.
We exist and have our being
In an intangible sea of thought.
We live in this sea
As a fish lives in water.
Floating in this sea for the taking
Is all the wisdom of the ancients.
Floating in this sea for the taking

Are all the aspirations
     of those now dead.
Floating in this sea for the taking
Are all the creative imaginings
Of the world's artists and prophets.
In this evolution
Each has a mission and a place.
We all contribute
To this sphere of the mind.
Thus our actions live on
Deathless through eternity.

          – Paul N. Carnes

Spring Solstice

Once more upon the cross the Life-God hangs
while Mother Earth, with chill autumnal breath,
surrenders to the barren sleep of death,
feeling no more her summer's fecund pangs,
Winter's sepulchral tomb gapes wide today,
Now grieving, let us lay him there, and then—
true to the mystery—keep watch till when,
at third moon's dawn, the stone shall roll away.

So ... well it is for us that in the faith
the resurrection's truth depends not on
belief in it—else were our souls a wraith
indeed, wailing toward oblivion.
But every spring life rises from its past
And so death too must change to life at last.

          – Leslie Blades

Vultures quartering a sky of passion drained,
Compute the first quick stab below of fear.
They register the synapses of pain
And smell the leakage of a crimson smear.

They spiral down the silken drapes of grief
And touch the wailing ground to bow their heads
Like mourners at a grave who stand and wait;
They also serve—by tearing death to shreds.

Dogs are barking across the gaps of night;
They sniff and lick the sores of Lazarus
And howl unhinged beneath a gibbous moon,
Returning to their vomit's incubus.
Tomorrow they will meekly stand to heel,
While raucous men knock roughened spar to spar,
Will wag their tails as others wag their skulls
Upon the gibbet shame of Golgotha.

Creatures of the rolling earth care nothing
For human tragedy; with wings they churn
The living air, and equally they shout
Hosanna! when the funeral embers burn.
But he, whose final sup is vinegar,
Whose agony has locked both heart and eyes,
Feels feathers of their flight across his breast
And hears the last long fracture of their cries.

– Leonard Mason

The Easter Miracle

I am amazed to the point of ecstasy
at the miracle of awareness.
Life brings me its freshness as an
      ineffable gift.
Every moment renews my vision.
Death is permission granted to other
      modes of life to exist,
so that everything may be ceaselessly renewed.
The ploughshare of sorrow,
breaking the heart,
opens up new sources of life.
The land bursts again into bloom.

The possible and the future are one.
The possible strives to come into being,
and can be, if we help.
Without sacrifice there is no resurrection.
Nothing grows, flowers and bears fruit,
    save by giving.
All that we try to save in ourselves
    wastes and perishes.
All things ripen for the giving's sake,
and in the giving are consummated.

– Jacob Trapp
(after Andre Gide)

Easter is Paradox

Easter is paradox;
It is the leap over the chasm
    between life and death,
Between victory and defeat,
Between joy and sorrow.

Easter holds together reality of crucifixion,
And myth of resurrection,
The Jesus of history and the Christ of Faith.

Those who lose their lives for others
    will be saved.
Those who save their lives for self
    will be lost.
Love is real only when we give it away.
Love hoarded melts inevitably as spring snow.

"In the midst of winter
(We) find in (ourselves) an invincible summer."

– Richard S. Gilbert

Poetry: Spring

Softening

O, it is softening . . .
The earth, I mean.
I know—I know:
I still see the snowflakes.
And dark skies;
I still feel the chill,
The chill-chill wind. But, O, it is softening,
The earth,
Softening toward spring.
Why, even now the goddess Eostre is impatient
  to be up and around
And sprinkling pinks and blues on bough and ground,
And Christ stirs behind the heavy stone at mouth of
  tomb:
Eostre, Christ, and all,
Restless to break through
Now that earth is softening,
Again.

– John Hanly Morgan

A Palm Sunday Admonition

To you who would as pilgrims go
With eager steps and hearts aglow,
When on the holy city bent
Be not deterred from high intent.

For people need triumphal days
With ample reassuring praise,
And palms extol while thorns do not —
And none would choose the martyr's lot.

So easy now to join the throng
With flow'ring branch and palm and song.
So hard to see on such a day
The beggar's hand beside the way.

How fine to do the pleasant deed,
To serve the current favored need,
But hope needs those who think and choose—
Uphold a cause they well may lose.

For those who would as pilgrims go
Both scorn and failure well may know,
And high intent can lead to pain
And gifts must never be for gain.

— Janet H. Bowering

(Can be sung to Tune: "Winchester New"
Singing the Living Tradition #145)

Green Thing

Green thing, green thing!
I see you - here, there
Tiny dots of green in spring
Along that tree limb, where
Birds, quick and bright, sing
Away cold winter's care.

Green thing, green thing!
Green on ground, snowless, bare:
I see you - here, there
Green on brown, tiny, fair.

Green in spring
Here, there,
And birds do sing.
And all is sweet,
And all is fair.

— John Hanly Morgan

When the daffodils arrive
In the Easter of the year,
And the spirit starts to thrive,

Let the heart beat free and clear.

When the pussy willows bloom
In the springing of the year,
Let the heart find loving room,
Spread their welcome far and near.

When the sweet rain showers come
In the greening of the year,
Birds will sing and bees will hum,
Alleluia time is here.

– Carl Seaburg

(Can be sung to Tune: "Hasidim"
Singing the Living Tradition, Hymn #62)

The Hurt of Beauty Healed

So rich in beauty is this earth
that when we contemplate its passage
down the arc of time toward
that inevitable dark where earth herself
must end, the hearts of all grow sick
with paradox,
and tongue and pen proclaim
a faith—shall not some deathless
spark transcending earth's demise
once more embark in quest
of beauty's meaning even then?

Shall spirit-eyes, probing
the mystery, find that the faith
eternally revealed is really
truth's supernal history wherein
the hurt of beauty can be healed?

And shall it not appear (as sometimes
seems) that timelessness was always—
now and here?

– Leslie Blades

Cosmic Cadence

In quick'ning streams and warming earth,
In buds and rootlets groping blind,
The world awakes and brings to birth
Eternal hopes to humankind.

The eons pass in cadence slow
Ideas through the centuries roam.
But all life forces blend and flow—
We harvest thoughts by others sown.

Each generation tries anew
And people venture to explore
Old wisdom clad in raiment new;
Fresh insight found in ancient lore.

A beacon from a far-off star
May touch a light-year distant soul.
A deed unmarked can travel far
And work to make a stranger whole.

Great good was wrought in ages past
When love and faith at wrongs were hurled:
So dare to change while life shall last,
Take hold and shake a dormant world!

– Janet H. Bowering

(Can be sung to Tune "Old Hundredth"
Singing the Living Tradition #370)

Birdsong

Good earth, good sky,
Here in the spring
I want to fly,
Take eager wing.

And roll and dive
Thru seas of light,
Come safe to limb
When it is night,

And hear the dark

All full of sound
And wake, and light
And peck the ground,

And lift again
Across the sky
And pipe a clear
Ecstatic cry:

"To-life! To-life!
Good-sky, good-earth,
Warm-wind, warm-rain,
Spring-birth, Spring-birth!"

– John Hanly Morgan

Aria for Willow

wind willow
silver in silver
rain
in February
promising spring

surprisingly silver
when sun-shot
a web suspended
on cables
of dawn

a mist in spring mist
a cloud
gold or green
dream of green or
gold

a mist
a wind
caught
wrought
in gold
a filigree of sway

weeping under
a weeping sky
April rain
streaming
greengold

— Dorothy Parsons East

Springtime

Late in February the sun brightens, the robins return.

The Pueblo Indians do their first spring dance "to bring the buds to blossom."

Then, within a few days, the first crocus is followed by many more, by white and purple hyacinths, by daffodils and tulips.

Leaf buds burst to a golden green. "Nature's first green is gold."

It warms toward Easter, when the second spring dance in the Pueblos helps "to bring the blossoms to fruit."

Early May will see peach, pear, apricot, and apple blossoms. My morning walks will be, going and coming, into the scent of lilacs.

— Jacob Trapp

Lilacs

tiny trumpets
pouring forth
a purple song

fragrance—
all of springtime
proffered at no price

lavender like
lavender hills
and white
and almost crimson

a brawling wind:
a surf of purple
flowers
against the wall

and everywhere…
purple winds crest and—
crash
in purple fragrance

– Dorothy Parsons East

Song for the Church Family

We take joy in many things
Thrusting shoots and silver showers.
Humming bee and bird that sings
Waking grass and opening flowers,
Find assurance as we do
In the beautiful and true.

With the people of all time
Wonder at the changing year.
Ancient ritual, chanted rhyme
Things we treasure, things we fear,
Find assurance as we do
In the beautiful and true.

Deepening roots and cherished lore
Mem'ries which all ages share
And for strangers at our door,
Warming welcome and to spare—
Find assurance as we do
In the beautiful and true.

– Janet H. Bowering
(Can be sung to the Tune "Dix"
Singing the Living Tradition #21)

Vocabulary Lesson

Awry in an otherwise orderly hedge
forsythia flaunts a golden edge
of sunshine, and thus by flouting reason
embodies the spirit of the season.

– Dorothy Parsons East

Goshawk

white winged ghost
whistling upon the crest
    of bursting branches
scrying messenger from the
    molten April sun,

belly specked with
reflections off snowpatches
    still tracked by fleet prey
    and awkward snowshoes.

I stand agape
    wishing wings.

– Ellen Dionna

In Praise of Spring

What courage pure with which we start
to gather fragments, bits, and parts,
with mindless grace that works and plays
and marks the season's passing days.

What cause in us to celebrate,
with calendar and special dates,
as we may try to comprehend
where seasons start, where seasons end?

What humaness to fix a date
and offer praise as if to bait
the inner growth we long to reach
that roots prepare and flowers teach.

What lesson wise on season's part
to pinch the mind but squeeze the heart
while pelting us with memories
of icy earth and naked trees?

What gift the bud, the growth, the flowers
that creep in spring and burst in power,

that cast our eyes in modest shame
and longing lust to do the same?

What flower's strength as if on cue
forgotten dreams that we once knew,
as winter wishes wake to sing
and feed the soul in praise of spring?

– Dawn Goodrich

IV. The Time of the Singing of Birds is Come

For lo, the winter is past,
the rain is over and gone;
the flowers appear on the earth;
the time of the singing of birds is come.

The Song of Solomon 2: 11,12

Responsive Readings

Easter

Rolling Away the Stone

In the tomb of the soul, we carry secrets, yearnings, pains, frustrations, loneliness, fears, regrets, worries.

In the tomb of the soul, we take refuge from the world and its heaviness.

In the tomb of the soul, we wrap ourselves in the security of darkness.

Sometimes this is a comfort, sometimes it is an escape.

Sometimes it prepares us for experience. Sometimes it insulates us from life.

Sometimes this tomb-life gives us time to feel the pain of the world and reach out to heal others. Sometimes it numbs us and locks us up with our own concerns.

In this season where light and darkness balance the day, we seek balance for ourselves.

Grateful for the darkness that has nourished us, we push away the stone and invite the light to awaken us to the possibilities for new life in ourselves and in our world.

– Sarah York

The Promise of Easter

Who is to say what Easter is that we should celebrate this day and sing for joy?

Easter is promises remembered and fulfilled of death and life and all that lies therein.

It is the promise of the planets in their turn, the infinite fidelity of stars and suns and seasons.

Easter is Winter promising to Spring that earth shall yield its death to life again.

It is the growth promise of the dormant seed, the barren meadow and the naked bough.

It is the birth promise of all creatures which have life and breath and being.

Easter is ancient sorrows stilled and hopes remembered. It is the memory of Jesus dying in Jerusalem.

It is the promise that his life shall never die as long as we still seek to dwell within his ways.

It is the promise that the heart shall be reborn as hatred dies and love is given birth.

It is the promise that the mind shall be renewed as ignorance is lost to newfound truth.

Easter is the promise to everyone who journeys from the death of prejudice to the life of understanding.

Easter is promises to everyone who casts away the errors of the darkness to dwell within the light.

Lo, Easter is of earthly promises and human hopes that make the human heart forever young.

A song of life which springs from death, a joyous human song, forever Alleluia sung.

– Eugene B. Navias

Easter Benedictions

Blessed be life!

Blessed be life moment by moment through a thousand ages!

Blessed be life that ends in every moment.

Blessed be life that rises again to blossom in every moment.

Blessed be life that remembers life.

Blessed be life that refuses to die before death.

Blessed be life that pours itself out into the mystery of the soul.

Blessed be life that becomes love, as the seed becomes the rose.

Blessed be life that lives its own amen!

– Mark Belletini

The Call of Easter

Easter calls to us out of the mist and fog, out of the melting snow and relentless rain of days past, and says to us—

> *Remember the sun of former days and the testimony of daffodils and forsythia to the golden moments of Spring that shall come again though we wait another day.*

Easter calls to us out of lost oppotunities and forgotten dreams that never came to pass, and says to us—

> *Remember that change is forever, that life ever renews itself at its own Spring, that new chances and opportunities are given out of the death of the old.*

A new self is waiting expectantly to come to birth within you,

> *To walk the earth once more with eyes that see, and ears that hear, and hearts that feel the glory and wonder of life again.*

Easter calls to us out of the hushed voices and haunting faces of those who have touched our lives and passed on to glories and mysteries we know not of. Easter speaks to us through them and says to us—

> *Remember the dead who are not dead so long as we have not forgotten them. To live on in hearts we leave behind is not to die, but to be reborn in the "life that maketh all things new."*

Easter calls to us out of the life and teachings of a prophet of long ago, whose form was crucified, dead and buried, but whose spirit rises up out of the grave and proclaims—

> *Though love be crucified it shall rise again in a thousand million hearts not yet born and in whose passion the power of love goes on and on.*

Though truth be nailed to the scaffold it shall rise again and bespeak itself in a still small voice that shall be heard above the harsh noises and clashing sounds of injustice and oppression.

Though a life of truth and love be shut up in a tomb, with the stone sealed in place, it shall rise again, the stone rolled away.

Walking the earth once more with quiet persistent footsteps

That shall be heard long after the sound of marching armies have faded into the night age after age.

Easter calls to us. Help us to hear it, see it, feel it. Unstop our ears. Uncover our eyes. Unseal our lips. Open up our hearts.

And let our voices sing, Alleluia!

– Richard M. Fewkes

Spring

The Wonder of Reviving Life

Who can resolve for us the mysteries of earth,
The wonder of reviving life in the spring!

Not all the stars in the sky are as wonderful as the bursting seed: or the tiny green shoot, or the first brave flower defying the storm.

The birds return, and in the dawn they form cathedral choirs rejoicing in the light.

The scampering squirrels take up the glad refrain, the Spring is here.

The trees sing in the wind, and little streams swell into leaping, laughing torrents;

The dead leaves nestling on the earth whisper a glorious secret to the wind: the earth is stirring with new life.

When yesterday the drifting snow covered gray leaves, impetuous green today thrusts upward toward the light.

All nature sings; for light is life, and warmth and rain are life.

This is the truth that passes understanding;
This is the joy to all forever free:

Life springs from death and shatters every fetter, and Winter yields to Spring eternally.

— Robert Terry Weston

The human spirit has its winter but it also has its spring.

This is the truth that must be retold each time the earth renews itself and restores our souls.

We know that impetuous green shoots and fragile blossoms do not alter the fact of sorrow and loss, and yet—

And yet we are uplifted again by the vitality and hope in the beauty of the awakening earth.

Only as we recognize the winter-like bonds which bind us and separate us from life—

Only as we open ourselves to light and warmth and growth can we set ourselves free.

Our intellect tells us that we are mortal and that we shall die later or sooner,

But our spirits tell us that we are one with the infinite, that some part of us will never cease to be.

— Janet H. Bowering

A Response of Hope

I looked to mother earth with a cry upon my lips, "What is your answer to the age-old question, 'If a person die, shall they live again?'"

And the earth was silent. Only a robin sang from the treetop and a crocus pushed its way through the leaves, lifting its face to the sun.

I gazed at the skies arching over my head, "O ye universes beyond universes, flying galaxies, and stupendous distances, what hint have you of our destiny beyond the rim of time?"

Silence from the darkening heavens. Only a whisper from those far-off worlds telling of wonders lying only as a dream in the human heart.

I flung my question down eons of time, "What is this many-splendored thing within our minds, coursing through our veins, flooding our souls and lifting our faces to the stars—this Something that cannot die?"

No answer came from out the vast tomb of the years; but the Spring flushed green across the ancient hills and something in the heart of April stirred—something that never dies!

I saw the evil and injustice under the sun and heard the bitter cries of human pain, the sad farewells at time of parting, and the universal query on our lips.

No answer came, but the surge of life went through the earth and filled the skies; eternal life and love which conquer death. Life-endless—triumphant! This many-splendored thing!

– Alfred S. Cole

V. Thou Givest the Grass

Thou givest the grass,
the corn, the tree;
seed-time and harvest
come from thee.

Mary Howitt

Readings

Ash Wednesday

Ashes and Easter

In a culture where the plastic smile is mandatory and cheap grace abounds, the sober subject of ashes comes almost as a refreshment. At least we know we start without illusions. All our minor triumphal entries end, like Lear, a ruined piece of nature upon the rack of this tough world.

The ashes of Ash Wednesday are mixed in a common bowl of grief. They are made from palm fronds used in celebration the year before at a brief hour of triumph, Palm Sunday. In the Catholic tradition the ashes are made into a paste and daubed on the foreheads of the faithful, a grey sign of execution that must preface any Easter.

John Bunyan said that the women of Canaan, who would not be daunted, though called dog by Christ (Mat. 15: 22) and the man who went to borrow bread at midnight (Luke 11: 5-8) were, ultimately, great encouragements to him. They hung in there thru the dark days.

For religious liberals ashes can symbolize, too, the dying of the seed that it may be born, the place of the phoenix, and, yes, the dissolution of integrity so that deeper integrities may emerge. The divine creativity leaves ashes in its wake so that new worlds may rise up and adore. In the strangeness of this business Ash Wednesday is the opening to Easter.

– Clarke Dewey Wells

Ash Wednesday

Teach us to care and not to care
Teach us to sit still.
—*T. S. Eliot*

I thought Ash Wednesday was the title of a poem by T.S. Eliot until I learned about the liturgical year in divinity school. One day I had a chance to learn more about Ash Wednesday.

It was a very, very busy day. I arose at 5:00 a.m. to catch a train from Southold, on the eastern tip of Long Island, into New York City, where I was scheduled to tape a television interview. A ministers' meeting was to follow the taping, then I would rush back out to Southold to meet with the Religious Education Committee.

O, my, was I busy! And important. It isn't every day, after all, that one gets to be on television. But I kept thinking of the rabbit in Alice in Wonderland who scurries around looking at his pocket watch, saying, "I'm late, I'm late, for a very important date."

After we taped the program, two of my colleagues and I left the CBS studio to make our way to the Community Church, where we were late for the ministers' meeting. As we bustled through the subway and the crowded streets, weaving around less hurried pedestrians, I realized that it was Ash Wednesday. I was reminded by the sign on the foreheads of many who passed us. What looked like a smudge of dirt was the sign of the cross made with ashes from palms blessed the previous year on Palm Sunday. I recalled not only what I knew of how the ashes are used, but also the verse from Genesis that is recited to each person as the ashes are rubbed on the forehead: "Remember … thou art dust, and to dust thou shalt return." Every time I passed someone with a smudgy face, I would hear the verse again: "Thou art dust and to dust thou shalt return."

I slowed my pace, lagging behind my companions, and paused to reflect that I was dust, already late for a very important date.

– Sarah York

Lent

Lent

What will you give up for this season,
to help life along
in its curious reversals?
As if we had a choice.
As if the world were not
constantly shedding us,
like feathers off a duck's back—
the ground is always
littered with our longings.

You can't help but wonder
about all the heroes,
the lives and limbs sacrificed
in their compulsion toward the good.
All those who dropped themselves
upon the earth's hard surface—
weren't they caught in pure astonishment
in the breath before they shattered?

Forget Sacrifice. Nothing
is tied so firmly that the wind
won't tear it from us at last.
The question is how to remain faithful
to all the impossible,
necessary resurrections.

– Lynn Ungar

I think the liturgical tradition of Lent is a gift, a garment for the storm, survival apparel. Our individual dyings and becomings are given a voice, wisdom, and companionship in a story and heritage larger than the isolation and pain of our unconnected selves. We don't have to be "religious" or "Christian" to enter into

Lent, only human. Since we're all in that club I invite you to join me in traversing together this season of faith, self-examination, and hope. We have St. Francis's word that "Brother Ash is pure."

– Clarke Dewey Wells

Lent

Forty is one of those numbers to which much significance has been given. Fortieth birthdays are often anticipated with dread. Many things can lurk in the "back forty." Forty also appears frequently in Western religious traditions: the forty days and nights of the Flood; the forty years the Hebrews spent wandering in the desert after the Exodus; the forty days from Christmas to Candlemas; and the forty days of Lent which precede Easter.

Lent is one of those liturgical seasons to which many Unitarian Universalists give little significance, and yet it may be the most "UU" of all the seasons in the traditional Church year. Its forty days signify a time for searching, exploring, pondering, evaluating, and taking stock of Life and one's place in it. It is a time of learning, expanding, broadening and deepening—of planting a new insight or discovery in one's daily living.

Taking time to acknowledge the ebb and flow of our lives is a good way to observe Lent: taking some quiet time for ourselves away from everything else, perhaps forty minutes a day just to sit and attend to whatever needs attention in our lives. Time to give up doing something else in order to take time to nurture something New.

Lent is perhaps best known as a time to give up something, to abstain from something—usually an indulgence of some kind. This is an idea which has some merit—for something new to take root and grow, we must first create and nurture a place where that may occur. We must consciously make room for the New, do a bit of mental/spiritual Spring-cleaning. For some, there already may be such a place waiting, even longing to be filled. For others, there may be so much filling them that it might be difficult, even painful, to let go of some things so that an empty space can emerge.

Lent can be a time of opportunity—opportunity that in the days to come, as the daylight continues to lengthen and the Earth begins to thaw, there might be a corresponding lengthening of Light within and a melting of our resistance to the astonishment that is the Life in All.

– Daniel E. Budd

"...anoint your head and wash your face..." Jesus

The Teutons of ancient days, after the long hard winter, rejoiced when the season's cold began to pass and the promise of spring was in the air. They held joyful festivals and sang praises to their gods. The "lengthening days" were for dancing and feasting.

Then the ponderous councils of the church moved in and proceeded to take the joy out of the season by prescribing that Lent be for self-denial, sackcloth and ashes, and a short-cut to holiness.

We should do better. Lent should be a season not of gloom but of cheer, not sulphur and molasses, but maple syrup and raised doughnuts, a time to celebrate the goodness, the beauty, and the utility in life.

Lent is a time not for monastic introspection but for expansion of mind and heart, for vigorous exercise and deep breathing, a time for getting the whole self tuned up so it can function harmoniously with the forces that lift the tulips and make the grass grow. It is a time for becoming more alive, for making love with your mate, and getting acquainted with your children.

– Clinton Lee Scott

Lent

If your yard looks anything like ours this opening of March and beginning of Lent, it is a mess. Broken tree limbs and twisted twigs from a dozen windy winter storms, mounds of crusty snow here and there like leftover icing shoved aside on a birthday cake plate. Bent over chrysanthemum stalks in the front flower bed, and all about there are soggy leaves—evidence of Autumn's unfinished business, abandoned with the first snow.

March, anticipating Spring, is a time to clean away the mess, the debris, to gather up and to restore. It is work, but a happy work on these dreary days if one can recollect the refulgent summer. It is a work to which one can whistle and hum.

Lent, anticipating Easter, is also a time to clear away the mess, the debris, to gather up and to restore. Lent is soul-work, or should be. It is a season to remove the dead twigs and leaves strewn about the ground of our being and to let the warmth of the sun get at those crusty patches of coldness which blemish the soul. Its purpose is to get to the core of the self. The medieval mystic, Meister Eckhart, said: "To get at the core of God at his greatest, one must first get into the core of himself at his least. Go to the depths of the soul: for all that God can do is focused there."

We modern folks have never taken much to Lent. Maybe it is because if we see something that is messed up we are apt to believe it is ruined. Somehow we are led to believe that the intrinsic value of a thing is not worth the time and skill for its restoration. That work we are apt to call drudgery.

Lent, however, affirms the intrinsic value of each soul. And if you affirm its value too, its supreme beauty and worth at the core, then you can see the necessity for the discipline for its care. Then this discipline, like picking up twigs and bundling them, can be done with whistling and humming. It means getting at the worth of the self, sorting out what is dead and gone by nurturing what is left and to come. It means centering in on the most important and clearing it away from the debris of dull routine and habit.

I hear complaints often that the hymns and themes of Lent are dull, drab and funereal. Yeah. So's our lawn—dull, drab, and funereal this time of year. And so's the soul this time of year, more likely than not. But the work of human restoration, like earth's restoration, should not be a time of gloom, but of whistling and humming.

– Bruce M. Clary

Palm Sunday

Palm Sunday

And when he drew near and saw the city he wept over it, saying, "Would that even today you knew the things that make for peace! But now they are hid from your eyes."
– Luke 19: 41-42

Imagine how Palm Sunday might have been experienced by an average citizen living in Jerusalem. A ten-year-old, for example …

It was the Jerusalem tourist season. People were coming into town from all over for Passover week. Boy, did I hate the crowds! My folks owned an inn and all people did was complain about the straw in their mattresses. I went out on the edge of town to advertise for the inn, and I saw a bunch of people coming toward me all shouting and gathered around a colt. Then they took off some of their clothes (that's what really got my attention) and put them on the colt. I wasn't really surprised. Those country folks always act a little odd when they come to the city. Then they put a man on that little colt. I was worried the poor animal might collapse.

Then people started throwing more clothes and some tree branches in front of the man and they called him a king. "Hosanna in the highest!" they shouted. He looked about as much like a king as my little brother. And high is not what he was on that colt—his feet were almost dragging on the ground. I knew my parents would be furious, but I decided to get into the parade and see why this man was being called the messiah.

According to everything I had learned about the Messiah, this guy did not make it. The messiah was supposed to be like David and Solomon. King David was a great warrior, a brave soldier. This man didn't even have a slingshot, as far as I could tell. And when someone made fun of him and threw a rock at him, he didn't say anything. I thought he was a real sissy, but then I followed the parade on into town where he went into the temple. Well, there was a big sale going on and he saw how some of the priests were overpricing stuff. He got real mad and said that they shouldn't be cheating people in God's house. He acted like he owned the place, which didn't go over too well with the priests. In fact, he made a real mess, turning some chairs and tables over. After that, the priests were out to get him, which was too bad, 'cause as far as I could tell, all he did was tell them not to cheat people in the temple.

One thing that was real obvious to me was that the people who put that man on the colt knew that he had some kind of power. You know, real power, like from God. And the priests knew it too, but they knew that his kind of power wouldn't go with their kind of power. Here he was with no horse and no weapons and no army so his power wasn't like King David's. And he couldn't afford a place to stay in the city, so his power wasn't wealth like King Solomon's.

Some people say he will return again some day. But I bet they wouldn't recognize him if he did. Because he would still have the same kind of power. You'd think that with that kind of power, people would recognize him, but even the ones who say he was the messiah don't want to give up the kind of power that

David and Solomon had.

Why is it that people say they want God's power, but when they experience it, they don't really want it after all?

— Sarah York

Good Friday

Good Friday

The Good Friday side of life
is where we find each other
touch each other
& realize
we are not alone alone.

— Ric Masten

"And when the sixth hour was come, there was darkness over the whole land until the ninth hour ... "

And after the ninth hour, when Jesus had cried out and given up his spirit, those that loved him came, and stood near to where the three were crucified. And they put up a ladder to take Jesus down and a wind came up and began to blow the dust about on the bald hill. Bracing themselves against the wind they worked to free his arms from the cross. Despairing, they found no gentle way to remove the nails. When finally they took him down, they laid him tenderly on a cloth and wrapped him with spices as was the custom, and carried him to the tomb which Joseph of Arimethia offered. Then those who loved him knew no promises kept, no future to be hoped, and they wept. But no one came to take down either of the thieves who perished also, and they were left to the winds and darkness of that place.

— Orlanda Brugnola

Meditation on the Rock of Sisyphus

Many a rock is pushed from the entrance of many a tomb by the force of the human spirit.

The rock is pushed away from the tomb of silence by the courage to speak when others hold their tongues and lose their conscience.

The stone of superstition and delusion is split in two by the clear thought of reason.

The boulders of dead habit, set in place by many years, are rolled aside by the quickness and newness of imagination.

The crags of inequality and selfishness are set astir by the piercing cry for justice.

The brick walls of indifference and callousness are eroded by a single tear of sympathy and cracked by the warm smile of kinship.

The dry gravel bed of vanished hopes is washed over by the waters of new possibilities.

Many a rock is pushed from the entrance to many a tomb by the force of the human spirit. Many a dark wall is washed white by the milk of love!

– Leroy Egenberger

Passover

L'sho-noh ha-bo-oh bee-ru-sho-lo-yeem.

May Zion be blessed with peace, and may our brethren and all humankind live in harmony and contentment. Amen.

—Benediction from the Passover Haggadah

The Jewish festival of Passover is known as "the Season of Our Freedom." Recalling their ancestors' release from bondage and oppression in Egypt, the people celebrate liberation. As the earth is released from the grip of winter, humanity celebrates release from bondage.

But the story doesn't stop with release. After terrible plagues and the exodus from Egypt, Pharaoh's army chased the people to the Red Sea, where the waters parted for the Hebrews, then flowed back to swallow up the Egyptian soldiers and their chariots.

Entering the wilderness, the people complained ("murmured") to Moses that it was his fault they were in this awful place, hungry and tired and thirsty.

This was only the beginning. The people murmured a lot in the wilderness. They recognized that bondage had been pretty secure. Life in slavery was a drag, but at least they knew what each day would bring, and a few conveniences had made their burdens easier to bear. Freedom sounded great when they were slaves, but now that the people had to set up camp and find food in a strange land, they weren't so sure.

It is safer to stay where things are familiar and events are predictable. It is safer to be in bondage. Freedom means risk; it means pursuing a dream of a promised land that we may never reach. One Jewish legend tells that even after Moses said words to part the sea, the waters did not recede until the first Hebrew placed a foot in the water.

The Passover Seder is a thanksgiving meal—a time to express gratitude to the God who hears the cries from all who are oppressed and exploited. It is a time to express regret for the suffering of all who pay the price for freedom, including those we call the enemy. And it is a time to express commitment to a vision of the promised land. For in the ritual of gratitude and remembering comes cour-age—the courage to put our feet in the water and take risks again and again for freedom.

– Sarah York

Easter

Easter summons us to life through death, not the abolition of death, not some impossible prolongation through endless time of an individuality that is dwarfed and distorted if it remains the same here and now through any extended period of time. There must be change, there must be growth, there must be imperma-nence. And death, however absolute it may appear when peered at through the keyhole of one individual's self-centered hold upon biological existence, is in fact but one great and awe-inspiring instrument in the orchestra that celebrates ever-lastingly the triumph of life.

– Phillip Hewett

We are the Resurrection and the Life

The resurrection stories of the New Testament need neither be taken as fact or reinterpreted to appear scientifically acceptable. They can be left as they are: myths of meaningfulness. They are the poetry of reverence. They are the stories of the reaffirmation of life that even death cannot end. They are the songs of the expe-rience of a people, who having experienced grief and loss and disillusionment, felt a restoration of their hope.

Human death is real. It is not at all similar to the retreat of plant life to the root to wait for spring. Human death is the end of life here, now, and among us. While a spring festival can crudely hint at the revival of life with the coming of crocuses, trillum, and bluets, our dead do not come back to life and show them-selves to us, their disciples, except in the intangible ways in which we are the return of the lives that have ended. We are the bodies that give their spirits flesh again. We are the specific forms of the life-force in the world, a force that seems to die in us in our winters and come to life again in our spring-times regardless of the time of year.

In us are written, if they are written at all, the new versions of the old story of Easter, the empty tomb, the renewal. We are at least part of what the ancient myth can mean, for we are or can be the resurrection and the life.

– Max A. Coots

Out of the depths of the experience of death and despair comes resurrection— unexpected, but possible, Easter is the power of inner rebirth that breaks the powers that hold us in bondage. It is the eternal "yes" that shatters every "no."

Out of the experience of slavery and persecution comes release, new freedom— unexpected, though longed for. Passover celebrates the reality of the New Day of justice, peace, and hope that has lived for centuries in the heart of humanity.

Out of the dreary days of winter comes spring—expected, but not without surprise. Easter marks the power of life's renewal built into the cycle of birth and growth and death on this our blue planet Earth.

May the spirit of rebirth, of freedom, of release, be with you all this season.

– Frederick E. Gillis

The surprise so powerfully portrayed in the resurrection story is this—our growing edge is not success, but failure. We can know what friendship means only when we have experienced rejection. The best counselors, I believe, are those who have had emotional problems themseves and have worked through them to health. The individual who has had a consistently successful and easy life is apt to be shallow, narrow, and obnoxious. For what we call "character" in a human being is determined largely not by how we handle our successes, but how we handle our failures. Personal growth requires setbacks. As one psychologist put it, "Ecstasy without agony is baloney." Resurrection without the cross is meaningless. In the nature of things, a lack of a cross is not a problem for most of us. For life does not consist of one success after another but is laced with problems, accidents, mistakes and failure.

– Charles S. Slap

Easter Week 1982

The light green shoots of blossoms-to-have-been are out of sight under the drifting snow. Gale force winds are rattling the old house. The temperature is far below freezing. Nature is not cooperating with preparations for Easter.

The storm evokes the spiritual quality of Good Friday more than Easter. New life will appear, but not without strife, not without some losses to the coldness which returns as inevitably as spring. And who can say that the sun will always climb again on Easter morning? Isn't it at least possible that the coldness has more staying power than the warmth?

The seasons are more reliable in these matters than human nature. For we, individually and collectively, can choose between love and indifference, between commitment and self-absorption, between peace and war. And we have often chosen the coldness.

Maybe the ancients were right. Maybe the spring comes because we bid it to come in our celebrations. Maybe it is the telling and the retelling of the stories that enable us to see that hope still lives and that we can carry it forward.

The stories make it clear that God does not do it alone. The motions of the spheres will produce a sunrise, but the springtime of the spirit, the springtime of love and justice and peace, depends on our human response to the gift of life.

Let us tell the stories again.

— Robert R. Walsh

The importance, for us, of Jesus, lies not in the way Jesus was born, nor in the way he died or supposedly rose again from the dead, nor in any of the miracles he supposedly performed. The importance of Jesus, for us, lies preeminently in the way he lived. And, similarly, I think most of us look to Jesus not as a Savior, not as the one and only Messiah, not as the King of Kings, the Lord of Lords, but as an exemplar—as an example of how to live a good and holy life in a troubled and brutal world. We look to Jesus not to lead us up to salvation, but back to ourselves.

— Andrew Kennedy

Blessing the Blend

The sentence, "May we bring ourselves and our stories to church this morning, and consider the blend a blessing," appeared twice in our Palm Sunday service yesterday. I always believe what I say on Sunday morning, but I said this prayerful sentence in particular earnest, having lived through a lifetime of Easter and Passover seasons in Unitarian Universalist churches.

Every year I fight the feeling that our UU churches just can't win on Easter. Our familiar congregation will come through the doors, alongside a number of

Easter visitors we've never seen before. Why do they come?

To hear familiar, traditional, Easter music.

To **not** hear familiar, traditional, Easter music.

To be reminded of the newness of spring, the pagan symbols of the season, and the lengthening days, without a lot of talk about Jesus and resurrection.

To be reminded of Jesus and His Resurrection, without a lot of talk about the newness of spring, the pagan symbols of the season, and the lengthening days.

To participate in a family service, where children delight in discovering the many roots of our religious tradition.

To participate in a dignified service, where adults celebrate the undeniably Christian holiday, Easter.

We each have religious stories, spring dreams, seasonal celebrations. And on Easter they're with us, joining together in church. It is our glorious celebration, and by considering the blend a blessing, we win every time.

– Jane Ranney Rzepka

The conventional Easter parable points to the life resurgent in nature, the "annual resurrection." Yet this triumph of life does not banish death. It embraces death. Much of last year's carnival of green, which celebrates the triumph of the spring, now lies in death and decay as the source and sustenance of the new and vigorous life which repeats the cycle. Nature is immortal, but her individual members are not. And it is only when we lose our craving for self-sufficiency, for an individual existence in isolation from, or even in opposition to, the great whole of which we are part, that we have really absorbed the lesson of this parable. Then we cease to live for ourselves alone, and begin to understand what it can mean to die and come again to life.

– Phillip Hewett

Bloom When the Snow Flies

The wind blows and the snow flies outside my window as I put pen on paper to think about Easter. It's an April bluster, another April Fool's trick of nature to make us think that spring won't come after all. But it won't work. Driving in my car today I saw the forsythia in full bloom, radiant golden yellow, ready to shout praises to the sun when all this blows over and light streams forth again in the morning. Believe me, when I tell you this, **Eastre,** the goddess of spring and renewal, will make her appearance this year. You can count on it.

What's true of outer weather is true of inner weather as well.

Whatever your losses—whatever in you is dead, frozen, rigidified—you've got what it takes to weather the storm and come through the other side of Good Friday to the resurrection of Easter. Hear the message of Easter. Jesus' spirit is risen today as it is each year at this time in the Christian calendar of worship. It was impossible to keep the influence of his life and teachings locked up inside a tomb forever. There was something eternally significant in what he said and did that burst the confines of his local history and habitat. He taught and modeled the power of sacrificial love and forgiveness and gave birth to a new epochal consciousness which continues to transform history. He belongs to the ages and his influence is still felt wherever the human spirit is renewed in the power of faith, hope, and love.

What's true of Jesus can also be true for you. If the spirit of Jesus can rise from the tomb of suffering and death so also can the human spirit in you arise to new beginnings and transformations without end—yearly, monthly, daily. You don't have to call yourself a Christian to believe this. You only have to be in touch with your own spiritual depths to know that it is so. Deep within your soul an inner sun is waiting to shine through the clouds of discouragement, pain, and sadness. The breakthrough won't always come when you want it. Spiritual renewal has its own period of unfolding and not always in concert with the cycles of the seasons. Joy can still come in the morning, but not until the mourning is over. Whether it comes early or late be assured that the forsythia can bloom radiant golden yellow in your soul whatever the season, even when the wind blows and the snow flies. You can count on it.

– Richard M. Fewkes

Resurrection

The resurrection isn't the only supernatural event in the Easter story. The disciples of Jesus lived in a world of the supernatural. According to Matthew, when Jesus died, the earth shook and coughed up corpses all over and "many bodies of the saints who had fallen asleep were raised." After the resurrection of Jesus, these saints showed up in Jerusalem. Well, if just by dying Jesus could empty all those tombs, maybe his own empty tomb was no marvel.

No, in a world where spirits rose up on a regular basis, there had to be something more special going on than just another corpse walking about. This was a resurrection of many souls, not from death, but from deadness.

What do I mean by deadness? I mean the things inside that kept the disciples away from Jesus' funeral—fear, cowardice, lack of conviction and purpose. And I mean those same things in our own lives that prevent us from feeling alive—things like fear, cowardice, and lack of conviction and purpose. And things like the loneliness, grief and boredom that numb us to life.

It's as if we let parts of ourselves die and stuff them away in a tomb of the soul. Sometimes that tomb is not such a bad place. It is like a womb—safe and secure, comfortable and predictable. Our tomb-life may be nothing more than the safety and comfort of a nice predictable routine. Or it may be a shelter from the world and its problems—a place to hide from the Jesus who called for a world where people care for one another. Whether it is escape or comfort, the time comes for us to roll away the stone and come out.

– Sarah York

When I Go To Church on Easter

...When I go to church on Easter, I expect to be reminded of the elemental truth that in this universe of ours, with all its hesitancies and timidities and tragedy, the tides of life are flowing "fresh, manifold, and free," and I expect to find myself swept into participation in the universal chant of praise for the irresistible, shining glory of the great gift of Life, which, for a brief moment and in an infinitesimal degree, I have the privilege of sharing.

– Frederick May Eliot

Easter Day

There is perhaps no day in all the year so full of meaning to the sensitive soul as the Easter Day. To say nothing of the beautiful music and flowers with which it is honored, it is to multitudes the anniversary of new life by which they were borne to higher ideals and nobler hopes. The peal of Easter bells and the melody of the Easter songs are the signals for a throng of memories and a host of suggestions to every heart. The origin of the day is simple enough. It is the anniversary of the Master's resurrection. But what are its deeper meanings, its profounder suggestions? I know not how it may be with you, but for myself they are embodied in such phrases as these: "Victory from the ashes of defeat;" "Hope born from the soil of despair;" "Immortality crowning the grave." The resurrection of Jesus means all this and more.

– George Landor Perin

"He is risen" (Matthew 27, 6)

Jesus is risen from the dead.
The centuries have not been able to bury him.

Forsaken by his friends,
sentenced to die with thieves,
his mangled body buried in a borrowed tomb,
he has risen to command
the hearts of millions, and
to haunt our hate-filled world
with the restlessness of undying hopes.

The years bring him increasingly to life.
The imperial forces that tried to destroy him
have long ago destroyed themselves.
Those who passed judgment upon him
are remembered only because of him.

Military might and political tyranny
still stalk the earth;
they too shall perish,
while the majesty of the carpenter-prophet
bearing his cross to the hill
will remain to rebuke the ways of violence.

– Clinton Lee Scott

The Dividends of One's Hope

If nothing else, Easter is a season celebrating the dividends of one's hope. It is not a celebration of hope itself, but of its first fruits—early blooming flowers, budding trees, returning birds. Endlessly without fail, the natural world renews itself following the barrenness of winter.

And, too, in the less tangible world of human emotions, we are periodically renewed. Out of tragedy often comes a chastened spirit; out of hate, an ability to love. Beneath the myth and ceremonies of every land and culture, this seems to be the message of the season. Take heart! For hope inevitably will bring about a springtime in the human spirit.

– Carl J. Nelson

Easter Meditation

Based upon a Statement by Robert Bellah

THE DEEPEST TRUTH I HAVE DISCOVERED IS
IF ONE ACCEPTS THE LOSS

of what has been ...
a friendship or an understanding
way of life or beloved person
for reason gone away

IF ONE GIVES UP CLINGING
TO WHAT IS IRRETRIEVABLY GONE

pretending it is not lost
or refusing to live any other life
than what we had with
what can never be or
be lived with or in again

THEN THE NOTHING WHICH IS LIFE

you without that friendship
or person or place
or feeling—you as you are now,
life as it presently is

IS NOT BARREN BUT ENORMOUSLY FRUITFUL

new things happen, new growths take place,
fresh strengths, greater understandings

EVERYTHING THAT ONE HAS LOST COMES
FLOODING BACK AGAIN OUT OF THE DARKNESS

memories, dreams, enjoyments,
sounds of a voice, touch of a hand
come back brilliant and alive,
come back as glorious parts of life

**ONE'S RELATION TO IT IS NOW –
FREE AND UNCLINGING**

You can go on, live with the past,
taste that part of life that was lived
but also create an untried life
without denying the relationship as it was
you can be free and unclinging in change

BUT THE RICHNESS OF THE NOTHING

when what you loved has gone,
and there are few familiar markings

**CONTAINS FAR MORE,
IT IS THE ALL-POSSIBLE
IT IS THE SPRING OF FREEDOM**

we can be true to the past
without being its prisoner
we can embrace the present
it is all possible
we can move into the future with hope
and even expectation.

                                      – Rudolph Nemser

Arthur Foote was fond of saying that Unitarian Universalists were theologically tongue-tied. By that, he meant that in our relationship to language and theology, we run the risk of talking only in vague abstractions about issues that might otherwise have great meaning in our lives. We need to have a religion that also evokes our feelings.

Easter is an excellent time for us very rational religionists to test ourselves in this regard. Too often we critique the theology of our neighbors (whether we believe it or whether it is believable) and we miss the opportunity that Easter affords our deepest selves.

I can't tell you if the resurrection of Jesus actually took place, and I certainly won't debate the issue. For me the Easter story speaks volumes anyway. It points to a more metaphorical "resurrection"—it's about the recurring presence of rebirth in each of our lives.

The date and details of Easter were not set in the early years of the Christian church but hundreds of years later by the Council of Nicea—the same council that declared Unitarianism to be a heresy.

Before that many churches celebrated a kind of Easter every Sunday, each week reflecting the potential of renewal, the metaphor of resurrection as we suffer small deaths in our despair, rigidity, and the ruts in which we too often find ourselves. This message was well received, for every life has many deaths and rebirths. Loosely defined, each of us knows, metaphorically at least, many crucifixions and resurrections during our lifetimes.

So let us ignore, nay even reject the implications of Easter which bind us with words and theology. Having been heretics for centuries, we are free to define Easter as we find meaning in it. For us, it doesn't matter whether the story of the resurrection of Jesus told at Easter is historically true or not.

We are called to stories not solely because of their verification. Rather we let stories into our lives because they contain a meaning or message that speaks to our lives.

It's been said that: "In and of itself Easter can do nothing for us. The day serves only as a reminder that if we will it, life can begin anew." It is not a simple assignment to change our lives, to transform the physical into a spiritual self. All this holy day can do is to declare: "It can be done."

– David Boyer

The Easter Nonsense

Easter makes no rational, logical sense at all. The Resurrection, "Christ the Lord is Risen Today," makes no sense. The concept of Eternal Life wins few converts from us moderns.

So why do we celebrate Easter? And why should Easter command the largest attendance of the year in our churches?

Let me suggest it is precisely because Easter does make no sense! And, because it makes no sense, we learn something.

We believe in Easter because we need it, deep down, for the good of our souls. Something in us urges us to believe that the sacrifices of love and works endure beyond the grave. Something in us urges us to hope our children will benefit from our worries and tears, our strivings and givings for them. Something in us urges that we and they shall be triumphant over our worldly fears.

Easter is a universal celebration because it is a natural response. My Dad says it's like the crabgrass that bursts through the concrete of his driveway. Concrete cannot contain the persistence of the fragile leaf of life. And it's like the lily which suddenly blooms out of a foot of snow. And it's like the soft word of comfort, no matter how clumsy, offered to one in deep grief. Suddenly there is the unexplained, irrational affirmation of life that wipes away all ugliness, gloom and despair. In whatever moment, it is known that life conquers death. It is always insistent and urgent.

Christ is risen in these moments because here is one life, which, illogically, shows us what all life can become—the inevitable conquest over death.

That is what all life is, really. Life well-received, well-lived, well-given, well-remembered, is life no death can destroy. And that, my friends, is the Life Eternal. It is Easter. And it makes sense after all.

– Bruce M. Clary

Some Things Will Never Die

The story of Easter and a resurrection, while not literally true, does point to a profound truth about life. That truth is that the darkest of times in the human spirit are succeeded by the renewal of life. Spring returning brings us that message.

Just as there is loneliness, abandonment, brutality, cruelty, hate, selfishness, fear, trembling insecurity, suffering and awareness of our mortality, so are there values and principles that cannot be killed. They may appear to be dead, but they rise again.

We see it in individual lives and in the lives of nations. Countries crushed under the oppressor's heel rise up to claim freedom and self-government.

Justice may be denied, delayed, twisted and corrupted, but it will rise again to be born anew in the hearts of people.

Truth may be crushed by tanks, armadas, official silences, but it will live again as it is kindled in the hearts of men and women who will live by no other standard.

Beauty is fragile. It may be surfaced over by highways or massive developments, but beauty rises to shine through to drive out the tawdry and ugly. Beauty cannot be killed.

Love may be buried beneath selfishness, cruelty, arrogance, and hatred, but the stone will be rolled away and love will rise again to walk with us, to inspire us.

Courage may be imprisoned in dank cells or the darkest of tombs, but courage springs up anew in the hearts of all the oppressed.

The power of human love to redeem human suffering and misery, to overcome fear and selfishness, to reach into the grave and beyond does not die. Beauty, Truth, Love, Justice, Courage live and inspire others and redeem human life when they are manifest in us and truly risen in our lives.

Some things will never die.

— W. Edward Harris

We're Not Sure What Happened

We received an invitation from our neighborhood newspaper to place an ad for Easter. Someone suggested to me that, should we advertise, it should say something like, "Join us. We're not sure what happened." I was tempted.

We're not sure what happened. But, we know what it's like when someone appears whose message we feel offers hope; who inspires us with new ways of living which touch our hearts and lift our spirits in anticipation. We know what it's like when they fall short of our expectations, or worse, are cut down by the forces of hate and bigotry which too often enter human life.

We're not sure what happened. But, we know what it's like when someone has grown profoundly into our own lives, who seems as much a part of our living as our own breathing, whose presence lives in our souls. We know what it's like when death takes them from us, perhaps prematurely, and the empty place now in our souls is much like an empty tomb.

We're not sure what happened. But, we know what it's like to feel sorrow and loss, despair, and grief. We know the waves of tears and the thoughts of the past which flow through us, which begin to fill the emptiness with stories and memories, begin to shore us up again with a different presence which will live with us for all of our lives.

We're not sure what happened. But, we know what it's like to realize, to have it dawn upon us, that what we have known and loved lives on now with and within us, a part of who we are. We know that somehow, in our hearts and souls, resurrection is real: not that of the body, but of the spirit—a spirit renewed, even reborn, in the midst of our lives and our living.

We're not sure what happened. But, we know that there is a difficult hope, a faith, that through the living of whatever sorrow and grief we feel (and will continue to feel on occasion) there is also a growing sense of grace and gratitude, of joy and thankfulness, in the mysterious and abiding astonishment of human being. In that wonder may we find our strength, our own sense of Easter.

– Daniel E. Budd

The Right Size

For years and years I bought the same size pants. I was convinced that I was a 36 inch waist. That was me. Sometimes we fail to take note of change. Once I lost about thirty pounds. Instead of realizing that the size of my pants would shrink with the corresponding weight loss, I continued to wear the familiar size 36. That was me. Now thirty pounds is quite a bit of weight, and so my pants began to look very baggy, and my belt was pulled to the very last notch. Then one day I was ordering some pants by mail order, and serendipitously wrote down size 34.

Many of us associate Easter with a time in our lives when our parents bought us new clothes to wear on Easter Sunday. There is symbolic meaning in trying on something new. The resurrection of Jesus and the springtime renewal of the earth both carry similar meanings. We can experience life anew if we cast off the habitual patterns of our lives. The potential for letting go of some anger or regret is present, but we are more comfortable sticking to our old ways of relating or being in the world. We keep saying size 36. That's me. The other day a package arrived in the mail. It was my pants. I was a little frightened of trying on this new size, but to my amazement, they fit beautifully. May Easter give all of us the courage to try something new.

– Mark W. Harris

Easter

A myth is not a tall tale. Quite the reverse. Whether it is true or false historically speaking, a living myth is true to *life*. The story of Jesus has lasted because it proved true to life after human life.

Daily, ordinary people show extraordinary courage. Grasped by some vision of a better life, a better world, they declare it and live by it, although bystanders insist the time is wrong, the idea is nonsense or worse, although there is no guarantee of a happy ending.

And all too often, there is no happy ending. Who has not cherished a dream that would not come true? Have we not all known the scourge of uncomprehending rejection, the pain of defeat? That pain is as real as the pain of the crucifixion. The death is real too: the irredeemable death of dreams. Yet there is hope beyond the grave, and meaning to the suffering. New visions can rise from the ashes, wiser and more compassionate ones.

There is meaning; there is value. Yet, when darkness surrounds us, it is hard to believe. At such times, let us turn to the tale of one who lived and died on such a scale that his significance is undeniable. The Easter story is our small passiontides writ large. So let this man's faithfulness till death dignify our own acts of faith. Did he die? … did he rise again? Let the truth of it rest within us, giving us courage, helping us hope.

– Joy Croft

The Story of Easter

The story of Easter is not simply a Christian story. It is true that for centuries the feast of Easter has celebrated the Resurrection of Jesus Christ. But the very name "Easter" is the name of a more ancient and non-Christian deity. The Easter season itself, since time immemorial, has been the occasion of rites and observances concerned with the mystery of life and death, resurrection and rebirth. Religions and races from all corners of the world have their special festivals of observances of what we call "Easter." As a result the full story of Easter is a most complex mixture of history and mythology, fact and fancy, theology and practice.

But underlying this matrix, there seems to be a persistent and common theme. The Easter story says that there is a destructiveness in life, a real agony and terror, an evil that is demonic; but there is also in life a renewal, a creativeness, and a persistence of goodness, even godliness. Easter says that often pain and suffering and sometimes destruction are necessary as the precondition of life and renewal.

To know inwardly the meaning of Easter is to be reborn. In truth, the only thing we need to fear is infidelity to the aliveness which we are and which surrounds us. For the growing edge of our experience is inexhaustible. This is the message which we have on highest authority: life has been tested and not found wanting on that first Easter morn. This we can know and depend upon all the days of our lives, in good moments and in moments when we face new Calvaries of the spirit. To be reborn at Easter is to understand, to know, to appreciate, to wonder, to pray, to roll back the darkness and despair by faith and courage. It is to venture by an inspiring faith in life's goodness which includes the recognition of life's evil. Easter is to glimpse the new morning, as sunrise on our way.

– Addison E. Steeves

Unitarian Easter

This tenderness which is the vernal Spring,
This hope of life—this poignant thing, this promise
Nature gives! Tremendous thrusting toward new birth,
Gigantic stirrings in the womb of earth,
Great with the cosmic urge
The bursting surge of life comes to new blossoming!
So let us live out our little days
That their rich seed may prosper
In the hearts of people,—that
We may thus be born again within the memory
Of friends our lives have touched,
Eternal Easter this, and surest immortality.

– Mary Stuart Komenda

Easter 1975

I'm having some dental work done at the Paley Clinic. The space in the clinic is cramped. I sit tilted far back in the dental chair with my dentist sitting at my right and his hygienist-assistant sitting at my left. As both were hovering over me—he drilling, she holding other instruments—her knee rubbed against my shouder. Having been injected with novocaine I felt no pain, only the relentless, steely attack pressure of the drill with its accompanying incessant and inhuman whine. I focused my attention on the knee pressed against my shoulder. The humanity of its warmth softened the moments and offered an escape from the destructive mechanical power of that cavity mining drill.

In those moments I remembered a fragment experience from my youth. A "flashback" to another dental situation—this time with my father who had been my dentist. I remembered sitting in my father's dental chair. As he worked he held my head close to his chest, tenderly cradling me although I must have been 12 or 14 at the time. I vividly remember his body warmth passing from him into me as he worked on my teeth.

We were not a "touching" family. We kept our distance. I recall no other instance where my father "took me in his arms." But the experience in the dental clinic chair brought back one of my warmest, closest memories of him. And with that memory came a resolve to touch **my** son (and daughters and wife) more often and more affectionately.

My father died fourteen years ago. He never knew what his "touching" meant to me. Neither did I until a dental hygienist's knee distracted me from the cold steel drill and helped me to focus attention upon humanity's warmth and tenderness.

The message of Easter is that even under the most dehumanizing and deadening conditions we can be "recalled to life." In that connection I suggest that the image of a dentist's chair provides a bizarre but not wholly inappropriate metaphor.

– Victor Carpenter

Resurrection

Sometimes Easter comes in Autumn. My friend Shirley called me the other day from Massachusetts to share a story with me. Ten-year-old Timmy came into her care from a program called "Mentor" which places emotionally disturbed youngsters in temporary homes.

She had begun to take children like Timmy into her home. Tim is non-verbal, but very bright and his story is a classic. He was abandoned by his mother at the age of three, raised by a few family members in succession who, each in turn, gave up because of his fierce temper tantrums. Finally Timmy was placed with his father, an alcoholic and abusive parent. Authorities suspect that Tim was badly mistreated, emotionally and physically by his father, and by his mother before that.

Shirley and her husband raise rabbits. Timmy, silent and morose, suspicious and not very cooperative, was put in charge of one of the pens. As the days went by, he became focused on his work with the rabbits, making sure they had plenty of pellets and enough water. Shirley watched him carefully and worked beside him—to make sure he treated the animals gently. Timmy made a special pet of one of the fluffy white does and he talked to her—but little more than he'd ever talked to human beings, who had lost his trust so long ago.

One morning last week, he came out to the pen with Shirley and his little doe had given birth. She was huddled in a corner and there, on the cage floor lay her three tiny babies—lifeless.

Timmy gagged in rage, and beat his fists against the sides of the cage, spitting out ugly names at his pet, screaming at her—"Why did you leave them alone? You didn't like them. You left them alone to die!" He cursed and cried, and scraped his fists on the wooden cage in desperation, "You left them, you left them alone."

Shirley reached into the cage with one arm restraining Timmy, and scooped three breathless lumps of skin into her palm, and ran to the house, pulling Tim with her, trying to soothe him with words and not let go of his arm.

She wrapped the three in an electric blanket—and an hour later Timmy stood wide-eyed watching the little doe's offspring squirm and wriggle in the warmth of the blanket.

Timmy has made his peace with the pet—and has lectured her more civilly on how to be a good mother. He talks more and more to everyone each day.

When I questioned Shirley about this miracle, she said simply, "Oh, rabbits are like that!"

So are little boys. So are the good people who take them in.

So is life like that.

— Marjorie Rebmann

Exultant

(This Exultant is to be interspersed between the verses of Hymn #78, "Color and Fragrance" of *Singing The Living Tradition*)

Tune of hymn is played, then:

I could say you are beautiful, you stars up there behind the sun!
I could say you give me pleasure, you red-painted moon and curve of comet!
I could say you ravish me, wisteria, narcissus, daffodil and tulip!
Or, I could say instead that you all seem lit from within,
brimming with something ineffable, something divine, something I could even call God.
But today I cannot say such things.
I cannot crucify words on the crisscross of competing cultures;
today I seem only glad to be alive, and crowned by marvels.

Vs. 1 and 2

I could say that the earth hanging in space is incredible.
I could say its an accident that just happened.
I could say it blossomed into being for no particular reason.
Or, I could say that it is commonplace miracle
in a cosmos filled to the brim with Godly miracles.
But today I cannot say such things.
I just cannot tell which word is which anymore: accident or miracle.
They seem to be twins.
And so today I rise in gladness again, and sing the marvel of it all.

Vs. 3 and 4

When some folks speak of heaven,
and others speak of earth,
for the life of me I cannot comprehend the seriousness of the debate.
Look. The heaven I see has no name,
just the silent sparkle of your eyes looking into my own.
And the earth I see has no name,
just scents I cannot explain to you and colors I cannot name.
In both the report of heaven and the vision of earth
I can sense intimations of a love so deep
it was once cradled only in the impossible word God.
But now I cannot confine such love in mortal words.
And so I am given over to song.

O Song beyond my songs, Song deeper than my inadequacy, brokenness or loss,
begin to sing Your immortal anthem in these mortal beings,
my sisters and brothers, alive now and yet. Amen.

Vs. 5 and 6

– Mark Belletini

Resurrection is real for all people—Christian or not—or it is real for none.

Jesus died. His death meant exactly what every death means: the end of his life's promise, the end of his hopes, the end of his dreams, and also the hopes and dreams which others had of him and for him—of what they hoped he was, of what they wanted him to be . . .

Something happened in the minds and hearts of Jesus' disciples, for whom everything had been lost. A transformation occurred, a radical shift from absolute despair to renewed hope, from a sense of the utter absence of Jesus to a feeling that in some way he was still with them. His death was not the end; it was the beginning. What had died became again lively in the world.

The possibility of transformation and renewal exists; it is in us. All around us are people whose lives, in ways large and small, have been transformed and renewed: those who have overcome the loss of what was most precious to them in the world, those who have won a battle with alcohol or others drugs, those who have transcended the temptation to despair when life was at its darkest. Resurrection is not a long ago, unique, unlikely event, but is potentially present in all human life. It is a promise and a challenge, for it represents the possibility of radical change—transformation—based on a radical sense of hope...

Death threatens us not only at the end of our lives but at every moment, the thousand little deaths of the spirit, the grievances we carry with us, the discouragements and sorrows that weigh us down, the sense of frustration or futility that darken our days and drear our nights. Easter is the promise that we can be reborn; it is the promise of new life. It is the assurance that in the midst of death we are in life.

The Easter faith can be expressed in two words: life wins.

– Earl Holt

Spring

Days

Some days my thoughts are just cocoons—all cold, and dull, and blind,
They hang from dripping branches in the grey woods of my mind;
And other days they drift and shine—such free and flying things!
I find the gold-dust in my hair, left by their brushing wings.

– Karle Wilson Baker

Spring

The spadefoot toad hibernates for months in the parched mud of the desert's
fire. Then suddenly with a rainfall in the spring the toad awakens and, like we in
this week, takes up a song. It is a song of celebration of the wetness and the toad's
existence, however brief. For it is both a love chant and a death knell. It is a song
which attracts the predatory coyote, owl, and snake. But still, in the face of dan-
ger, the spadefoot sings. Because it knows that even the coyote, owl, and snake
may offer the reflection of an angel's wing.

- William F. Schulz

The Green Laughter of Spring

I am struck dumb with wild and wordless wonder
That on this planet, hurtling 'round the sun,
The green laughter of spring rises to clothe
Our earth through cell and seed and birth –
Eternally, in spite of winter's storms and cold.

Through ages of fire and of ice the flow of life
In countless deaths and multi-million forms
Has known the con-fraternity and miracle of birth.
This, my miracle, my "resurrection of the flesh" –
Too vast, too true for little creeds, is spring's
Unbridled mirth!

– John Cummins

The Hesitant Spring

Spring is more than a month old now, but still occasionally the cold returns to catch us unprepared. The wind whips past us as we rush from car to home, glancing only briefly at the shivering daffodils and magnolia blossoms. We dare not pack away the winter coat, the sweaters and wool slacks that we have wearied of, whose weight holds us back from the dance of a new life.

So in our individual lives, change comes slowly, haltingly, grudgingly. Although we may feel deeply the need to discard old habits and tired patterns, still they clutch at us, crippling our tentative new steps, freezing us in movements that we once found comfortable but which we have now outgrown. Even as we yearn to be set free, to set ourselves free, we feel the temptation of the old and familiar. However painful and limiting, the old ways seem at times safer than the uncertain paths ahead.

These transitions are difficult: one step forward, the next one backward; yes, no; I will, I won't. And then one day the spring is here, no longer to be denied. Leaves and blossoms have all burst out and no longer fear the frost. We dance, fully and freely, enjoying movements and rhythms that before we could only vaguely imagine. O, splendid awakening spring, amazing metamorphosis, caterpillar turned butterfly, we hail your presence within and around us.

– Helen Lutton Cohen

Winter into Spring

The trees, along their bare limbs,
contemplate green.
A flicker, rising, flashes rust and white
before vanishing into stillness,
and raked leaves crumble imperceptibly
to dirt.

On all sides life opens and closes
around you like a mouth.
Will you pretend you are not
caught between its teeth?

The kestral in its swift dive
and the mouse below,
the first green shoots that

will not wait for spring
are a language constantly forming.

Quiet your pride and listen.
There—beneath the rainfall
and the ravens calling you can hear it—
the great tongue constantly enunciating
something that rings through the world
as grace.

– Lynn Ungar

The Colors of Life

Consider the amazing bulb flowers
—Hyacinth, Crocus, Daffodills—
Bulb resurrections sprouting in corners
of yards, fences,
In unexpected places though they
appear year after year.

Consider bulb ability to respond to the
mixed up weather,
Amazing force with which they emerge
and reach up to the sky—
Slicing through accumulated leaves and
earth not-long-ago frozen,
Springing up with joy to show their
colors.
Bulbs get on with the vital endeavor—
life.
Sometimes, they suspend their progress,
Chilled to a stop by the freezing winds,
Buds clenched tight for protection,
And then, sometimes, when the weather
warms or the rains quench,
Bulb plants surge upwards (you can
measure the growth in inches per hour),
Unstoppable in their rush to smile back
at the sun.

We, too, are equipped with that
inexorable drive
To show our colors, to fulfill our lives.
What coldness of mind or spirit keeps
our life restrained?
What deep freeze of doubt, or fear, or
numbness?
What layers have accumulated to thwart,
distort, or impede our thriving?

Be gardeners—peel back the thwarting
accumulation of old ideas,
Of untried impressions, habits, fears,
and unexamined doubts,
Revealing the struggling shoots of life,
and wait, wait,
Through wind and rain and cold. Watch
and wait,
For the warmth will come again,
Smiles will appear,
With surges of joy
The colors of life will grow into being . . .

All in good time, all in good time.

– Betsy Spaulding

Spring Is A Tide

Spring is a tide that rises in the human heart, and will not be denied! Each of us, like the small sea snail, builds our own shell of habit or illusion, erecting futile barricades against life. But then we hear the challenge from beyond. If a person does not answer by bursting through the shell, the little home becomes first our prison, and then our tomb!

Each of us is an animal that walks spiritually as well as physically, and to walk is to put the land of the safe and familiar behind you, to hazard all you are. This is the way of living, growing things, and it it is beautiful to behold. Spring is a tide that rises in the human heart, and will not be denied!

– John Cummins

Hawk Flight At Walden

On such a day as this, it must have been,
Thoreau walked at the edge of Walden Pond and smelled
The wet earth warming in the sun, the leaf-buds bursting,
Heard the striped squirrel chirp, the wild geese honk
       commands,
The very trill the word of its return. On such a day
He must have watched that tenant of the air the hawk,
Sporting with proud reliance on its satin wings,
Mount and tumble and fall and mount again
As if it had been hatched out of some nest,
Fashioned of rainbow trimmings lined with haze,
Pitched in the angle of a cloud, a bird not meant for
       earth
But for the wide pure curve and movement of celestial
       play
Whereby the witness who has mind to learn and eyes to see,
On such a day, looks up and knows himself forever free.

– Althea Bass

Awakenings

The book and subsequent movie, "Awakenings," depict the story of a group of people who fall victim to a disease whereby they "fall asleep" from once active lives, and have lived an apparent "zombie" existence for decades. During their sleep, brain activity has continued, but they are trapped by this mysterious disease. While most of us never know such a Rip Van Winkle experience, it does make us wonder what parts of life we sleepwalk through. The poet Kabir once wrote, "If you are in love, then why are you asleep?" The spring implores us to consider what sleep in our lives we might awake from.

    If we are haunted by our past, why not awake to live for
        today?

    If we are numbed by the effects of violence, why not
        awake to peace?

    If we feel isolated from others, why not try to
        speak our love?

In the story the victims of the disease find relief with the help of a drug. They suddenly awake to all the wonders the world has to offer. We have countless opportunities to wake up to what our lives have to offer. In "Awakenings" they are able to love and dance again with great joy. They are given a new life, and one responds by saying," I want to do everything." Sometimes when we are delivered from some terrible ordeal or even just feel happy with the onset of spring, we want to shout with new found freedom that the old burdens or the cold winter in our lives is over. Wow! I want to do everything!

– Mark W. Harris

Vernal Equinox

Winter washed away last night
And ancient fear, deep frozen in the
                    dark of time
Broke loose before the coming
                    spring.
The weight of ages melted under
                    mystic change,
And plunged the torrent of its spirit
                    out across the lands.
Bleak fingers, clutching ice, reached
                    up to hold the glacier back.
But suddenly
The dawn appeared and called
                    upon the sun of hope
To take its place within the human
                    heart.
The night was gone!
The morning came!
We stand new born to meet our
                    selves again
In earth's celestial change.

– Robert L. Zoerheide

For Eyes That See

May we have eyes that see!

Eyes that see the beauty of the earth and the glory of the skies; that reflect the light of dawns and sunsets and the valiant noons, and the stars at night.

Eyes that thrill to the poetry of trees, of grasses, and of flowers.

Eyes that delight in the gladness of the smiles that we can share; eyes that mingle their tears with the tears of those who weep.

Eyes whose vision reaches to far horizons and which see there the dim prophecy of what we yet shall be.

May we have eyes that see!

– Jay William Hudson

For deep below the deeps of human consciousness there is a power, a new being ever waiting to be born, a power of hope and faith and courage in the face of adversity, tragedy and loss, a power of love and endurance and venturing forth to new beginnings for young and old at all stages of human becoming. The power is within us and yet beyond us; accessible to us in our own faith response to the pain and glory of life; gifted to us in the discovery of momentary sources of strength and compassion, of joy and praise, we did not know were there. Resurrections here and now—multiple, diverse, recurrent, perennial. Alleluia!

– Richard M. Fewkes

Spring and Words

We meet together at a time when the earth is renewing herself peacefully, marvelously, victoriously. No power on earth may push back this triumphant tide of life. Truly the light is sweet, and a pleasant thing it is for our eyes to behold the sun.

As we respond to the joyful rhythm of this season, we are grateful that we ourselves are part of this great and glorious ordering. We know that we are maintained by the energy that awakens in myriad forms of life with a generosity that we may never fully measure or understand.

We are grateful, too, for the unnumbered processes within us which we do not have to control but which of their own accord, unconsciously, work together in harmony to make possible our lives.

All unseen, the goodness of the air blesses every cell and fibre of our bodies, while silently our blood circulates through our veins, food strengthens us, and water, so humble and precious and clean, daily bestows its vital blessings.

We remind ourselves that we are part of the ceaseless web of life, part of the harmony in the eternal song of praise: we resolve not to break, through stupidity, carelessness or greed, the lovely and delicate strands of life's web; not to bring discord and ugliness into the music of life. When we bring these things to mind, we begin to understand that in the divine will is our peace, for we sense that the love that rises so falteringly in us is linked to the love that moves the sun and other stars.

At the same time as we behold a vision of glory, we are ashamed of our failures and sins. We have the gift of awareness: we know when we have done wrong, missed the mark, strengthened the power of evil.

So we pray for the cleansing, healing strength of good will, that our powers of thought, imagination and speech may be well-used. We pray for the power to communicate, not in words alone, but in life. We have messages to give, welling up from the depths of our lives, living words that only we can speak, loving deeds that only we can do.

Grant above all, that our communications may be like the sowing of seeds, and that those who receive them may look to a fine harvest.

– Frank Walker

Precariously Perched on the Precipice of Spring

We are precariously perched on the precipice of spring, trying to shake from our spirits the coldness of snow. The heart's winter is releasing its iron grip upon us. We are poised in anticipation of a warmer time.

Do I speak only of the pageant of earth's seasons or do I mean the procession of the winters and springs of the heart? Even in the glory of reviving spring, the reminders of winter deaths are about us—the yard reveals the refuse of the months. It is not unlike the soul—sometimes it is buoyant with new life, sometimes strewn with the remnants of broken dreams.

The soul's journey is as unpredictable as the weather—temperatures rise and fall with steady mathematical precision and they also leap and plummet with rude abruptness. There is just no telling.

But while we may escape winter's icy hold on our bodies, there is no escaping the coldness of the heart. Mostly, life is not so much an arctic or a tropic clime, but a temperate one which knows both cold and warmth.

There is no escaping the seasons of life—we simply learn to live with them— bundle ourselves against the cold or find cool refreshment from oppressive heat. We learn to live with them, for like the seasons, they pass on and away. But how joyous to know that now, for a fleeting moment, we are precariously perched on the precipice of spring.

– Richard S. Gilbert

VI. The Soul Hath Lifted Moments

The soul hath lifted moments,
Above the drift of days,
When life's great meaning breaketh,
In sunrise on our ways.

– Williamn Channing Gannett

Prayers and Meditations

Lent

On this first Sunday in Lent, we are reminded of so many things, coming up to us out of our backgrounds—the history both of blessing and curse which has been the mark of Christianity through the ages—so much of it a denial of the wonder and grace of that Man of Nazareth whose brief ministry to his own people changed the world both for good and ill.

We would be reminded in the day that now is and in the weeks that lie ahead, of the task that each of us has of being a true disciple—disciplined, ordered, and yet free—free to roam with our thoughts and our impulses, our intention above all—to bring peace through out lives, to all whom we touch, and through that, grace and peace to all our world.

We know how difficult it is—we know how ego-centered we are, and yet, we would find in these moments of quiet together the power and the grace to be more than we have been, and more of what we might be, now and always.

So may it be.

– Philip Randall Giles

Palm Sunday

Thou who art the heart and soul of life, save us from fear, the fear of days and nights yet to be, the idea of the known and the unknown, the fear that builds high walls around our spirits and our lives, the fear that closes in and envelopes us, the fear that nibbles at the edge of every satisfaction. Free us from fear of failure and success, of shame and pain, of death and fear of life as well. Open our eyes that we may see Thy glory in humbleness and simplicity, commonness strewn generously across our path all our days. May we recognize Thee riding upon a simple beast of burden, down the crooked streets of Jerusalem. May we not require the palms of victory and praise, the accolades and shouts of the multitude to see Thy glory in gentleness, patience, loving kindness and, yes, pain and sometimes death. Thy way of peace, of faith, hope, and love still is our path, our joy, our way.

– David A. Johnson

Palm Sunday, 1964

O Thou, who art the holiness of Being itself, who dost appear to us in any of life's vicissitudes in accordance to our expectations, and who by thy grace doth fill our common moments, and even tragedies, with exultation and who doth chasten us with the constant reminders of thine omnipotence, we ask that Thou be present in our worship. As we celebrate the beginning of the Week of Passion of our Elder Brother, Jesus of Nazareth, may we, as he, not be tempted either by the applause or the condemnation of others but strive to hold on to that inner fire of integrity which can mingle in ever so delicate proportions the "independence of solitude" with "charity for all." Amen.

– Paul N. Carnes

O God of life and faith, be with us as we face life's Jerusalems. Grant us the courage to ride forth and meet them. Give us the wisdom not to be enamored by the "Hosannas" of the moment and keep us from bartering away our integrity. Rather, O God, fill us with a Christlike spirit. Take away our selfishness. Enlarge our vision; deepen our conscience; increase our faith. So may we become instruments of hope and healing in your world.

– Harry H. Hoehler

On this Palm Sunday morning, we look forward to the coming of warm weather and the budding of spring flowers, a respite between the hazards of winter and the heat of the summer. We look forward to the coming days of vacation for the restoration of our bodies and minds and to the renewal of strength.

With each new season we find new hope, a new beginning, a new vision for the future. That vision must be our own making. The choice of vision must be our own, and what we do with it and what strength and fulfillment we gain from our own capacities to reach beyond ourselves into the future must come from within us.

For, with divine inspiration and guidance, we must strive to reach beyond our present concerns to dare to address new hopes and new solutions to our struggles and to the struggles of all humankind.

Let us strive to form bold visions and to make bold and even daring decisions to heal our souls and to support the hopes and visions of each other and of suffering humanity.

Be with us this Easter season as we gather in worship and in the customary ceremonies of this week of hope. Give us hope, we pray; give us vision; give us right and useful decision. Amen.

– Priscilla Murdock

Palm Sunday prayer

We are thankful this day, O God, for the beauty of the earth renewed, for the loveliness of life and for its promise, and for everything that brings awakening to the soul.

We are thankful for all lives great and good, the memory of which can never perish, and the power and influence of which increase as we become more ready to receive them. We are thankful for those who in the mystery of life could find their path: those who in darkness lighted a lamp for others to see by; those who could bring to utterance the sacred insights of the spirit: those who have made more plain life's nobler way.

And we are thankful for those the goodness of whose lives was more than lesser people could suffer the reproach of: those who were faithful unto death. Especially we think of Jesus, who walked in Galilee, carrying the radiance of his vision with him and speaking simply to simple people so that they found new confidence and hope. And of Jesus whose mission grew and took him to Jerusalem, where the people who had known and loved him hailed him as their King.

Brief was his triumph, followed swiftly by his anguish! Yet we can hear hosannas still, echoing to us through the centuries, and when we remember him, love takes possession of our hearts,

In him, O God, Thy spirit was a pure, white flame. We shall never forget him; no, nor all the generations that come after. He has laid upon the ages the touch of his humanity; he has marked our pathway from Nazareth to God.

– A. Powell Davies

And so we come on our donkeys,
Some from Detroit and some from Tokyo and even a few from Seoul.
With horns blaring and brakes screeching,
We enter the city, the holy of holies.
We know what Caesar wants:
Testing ranges and new arenas while the homeless haunt church
    basements and the poor shuffle in the streets.
But we march to a different drummer.
Not many rich, not many mighty.
A vagabond crew in a strange land,
Whose ways are not our ways
Nor thoughts our thoughts.
But let us be of good cheer.
Let the word go out.
The donkey is mightier than the missile,
And flowers have been known to split a rock.
This week moves inexorably toward Friday.
It is Caesar's week.
But it is God's world.
And so we take heart and rejoice. Amen.

– Roger Cowan

Maundy Thursday

O God, you know our weaknesses, how confused and fearful we are. Our personal ambitions so often divert us, blocking us from your purposes for us. Help us to find our path again by instilling in us a Christ-inspired vision. Strengthen us with a Gethsemane faith so that in our praying and in our living we will seek not our indulgent ways but your ways of grace and peace. Keep us in your great care, O God, and make us faithful servants of your holy will. Amen.

– Harry H. Hoehler

Good Friday

We are grateful this day, O God, for all the sages, saints, and martyrs who have given of themselves to save humanity because the command was laid upon them. And towering among them, the Man from Nazareth, who in so short a time lived so much promise into life. We can see him still, and the brightness of his presence, coming to us over the centuries, his love still warms us, though the words in which he spoke of it were so long ago. And we remember how at last, reluctant to yield up so rich a life, yet willing if it must be, he went in anguish to the cross; and thus he won his victory.

We stand, O God, and marvel at so great a sacrifice. When will we receive Thy prophets and Thy saints? How long must love be crucified? We bow our heads and in the stillness of our thoughts there comes a new resolve: he shall live on! Our hearts will make him room! Until throughout the world such love as his has won its victory. Amen.

– A. Powell Davies

Almighty God, Giver and Preserver and Renewer of life, we would come in the fullness of joy, in the renewal of hope and strength and aspiration to worship Thee. We would feel that behind us and within us there is power not yet exhausted, there is life yet to be lived with fuller meaning and with gladder promise. We remember today all those who in ages past have lived, and wrought righteousness, those who have testified to eternal power through the renewal of their own lives, who have made this life of ours more pure and beautiful and strong. They have lived their lives, they have spoken their words, their works follow them. Still the new generations are coming on, and still the voice of childhood and of youth, with its high expectations and daring comes anew. The great adventure has not ended. And so we remember all those who have thus kept alive in human hearts the sense of the dignity and the worth and the divinity of life.

We remember Jesus of Nazareth, his life, his death, the great words spoken by him, the great ideals roused in others by the story of that life. And may we live in our generation with that sense of the nearness of the divine, of the tenderness of all that is human, of the grace and love made manifest through human personality. Amen.

– Samuel McChord Crothers

A Tomb is no Place To Stay: An Easter Meditation

A tomb is no place to stay
Be it a cave in the Judean hills
Or a dark cavern of the spirit.

A tomb is no place to stay
When fresh grass rolls away the stone of winter cold
And valiant flowers burst their way to warmth and light.

A tomb is no place to stay
When each morning announces our reprieve,
And we know we are granted yet another day of living.

A tomb is no place to stay
When life laughs a welcome
To hearts which have been away too long.

– Richard S. Gilbert

Easter

We know that, physically speaking, birth and life must come before death but we have learned that, spiritually speaking, anguish and death must come before Life. We thank Thee for all the men and women, known or unknown, who, because they loved their fellows and the common good, chose the difficult path of reprisal and condemnation. We would be reminded that the suffering so incurred is not binding or final but that a harvest of life always results from it.

In contrast, may we see that our easy and convenient lives are not so much the outcome of clear thinking as of selfishness and spiritual self-delusion. Help us to praise great souls, such as Jesus, who was one of those who planted suffering and death that we might reap life, not with our lips only, not simply to meet our emotional needs, but with our lives also. Sure in the knowledge that Thou Who hast lifted up all faithful workers for the truth, and lifted them out of shame and death, setting their humanity on high and making it glorious in the might of Thy Spirit, will also walk with us, if we should choose to walk with Thee, may we also contend for the right and, if need be, suffer for it, paying the price that men and women in every time and in every land have paid.

May the elevation of our hopes for man and the strength of our resolve to build a city of man on earth, be the marks of our resurrected humanity. May Jesus at last walk out of the tomb, as children are fed and healed and led in paths of self-fulfillment, as the vigorous poor find justice and opportunity, and as the elderly find someone who is sincerely interested in them.

– Gaston M. Carrier

Easter Sunday, 1964

O God, whose divine presence is everywhere manifest to those who remain open to its possibility, but which is most particularly apparent in the ever-recurrence of life, touch our hearts with the knowledge of thanksgiving, and our minds with the bright vision of hope.

And so, as we glory in the awareness of heights and depths of life as we have been blessed to live it, we would remember with compassion those who lives are cut off by illness to mind and body, or through malice, or through their own blind choice of evil-doing. May a heavenly alchemy mix our concern with their welfare, so that this day some sense of renewal may be born in their lives, as in ours, thus making answer to our prayer.

– Paul N. Carnes

God of Light, with whom is no variableness, neither shadow of turning, we look to Thee on this day of joy and gladness. The night has passed away, driven by the sun which uncovers the blue expanse of heaven and the glistening trees. So shall, through all ages, the war of light and darkness be, and so shall it end. Always.

This is the essence of the Easter message.

We must speak with our hearts lest we be strangers unto Thee. We yearn to make our lives a part of Thy wondrous plan, as belonging to those who care to help, who dare to speak for a more human world; lest we be as little babies who receive and enjoy without realizing the cost, to someone, of everything, and who want to take without giving.

This is the depth of the Easter message.

Allow us to see that our lives count crucially in the scales. If we give in to indolence and drop our obligations, then the whole world will be a little weaker; but the whole world moves forward, it may be by a very small amount, if we overcome our indifference and coldness of heart. Thou, Who alone hast the right to judge any person, receive this day, our affection and our gratitude with the promise of lives made lighter and brighter through service.

This is the thrill of Easter. Amen.

– Gaston M. Carrier

Easter

Lord, we have prepared for this day and waited long for its coming. On other Sabbaths we have whispered to thee our hopes and longings; but there are hopes and longings which only Easter Day can understand, and we have saved them for its coming. We beseech thee not to disappoint us but to be unto us, more than ever, a God who keepeth covenant and mercy with his people.

We have sought occasion to believe, with all our hearts, even that which seems impossible; to show the eagerness of our trust by the willingness of our credulity. But we have been checked by the disdain of our earthly logic, and chained in the prison-house of these earthly rationalities. Let this day, consecrated to thy Sovereign Majesty, strike off the chains and release our souls that they may rise to thee who art above every rationality, and unto whom nothing is impossible.

We have spoken farewell to friends and dear ones as they have obeyed thy last summons, and we have sought the only solace that our aching hearts could find in saying that birth and death are alike gifts of thy mercy, and that though hearts are dust, hearts' loves remain. But thou has seen how hard it is for its to accept the promise we so greatly crave. Let this Easter Day laugh away our doubts; and warn us of our fault—not that we expect too much, but that we do not expect enough. Forgive us for judging thy loving-kindness by our own, and for saying it is too good to be true—whereas, to thee, it is too good not to be true.

Let this day consummate its greatest blessing by teaching us humility and a saving distrust of self. Let it help us to make the venture of faith, to step beyond our self-reliance and place our reliance on a power and love we cannot measure.

So grant us, as those who have been chastened and blest, to gather ourselves together and discard our vesture of doubt and timidity, and fare forth upon our pilgrim way faithful and believing, hoping and rejoicing, sons and daughters of our King. We only ask thee to confirm what we have been taught by him whom no earthly sepulcher could contain. Amen.

– Charles Edward Park

Easter Sunday, 1969

On this morning when the returning warmth of the sun reminds us of our dependence, actual as well as felt, on the elemental sources of nature, and when the emergence of life and joy justifies the hope that sustained us through the winter, may we both know and affirm the glory and blessing of Creation in a renewed vision of holiness. How we speak of this, what words and signs we use, will bespeak our individuality of interest, taste, habit, and desire. Only let it be seen, that it may lay a claim upon us to the point that satisfaction be extended with duty, and we become not only open to others but steps whereby time may ascend over to us a more glorious future. And so, O God, may we be sustained in any present.

— Paul N. Carnes

Christ rose from the dead on Easter Day, we're told. To all who believe on him comes the promise of resurrection and eternal life. So the story goes.

We, in a less believing age, see resurrection as macabre and eternity as more time than we can bear. We believe, more modestly, in what we see— crocuses pushing through the ground while snow still fills the air, buds shoving their way out from dead brown twigs, wings in the air, heading south. We believe in what we feel—the soft fuzz of pussy willows, the warmth of sun on skin, the damp crumble of unfrozen earth.

It's time! Time to take off our coats, roll up our sleeves, plunge our fingers into the soil and breathe the fragrance of resurgent life. All flesh of the earth is new with green things growing. Look around: you just might see the earth in the act of eternity!

— Maryell Cleary

Eternal Spirit, sometimes when tragedy strikes I sit alone and weep. Take this cup from my lips, I ask. It is more than I can bear. But death happens, illness persists, prejudice continues, misfortunes multiply, cruelty abounds. At last, I know that this is my destiny, to carry these burdens upon my back for to do otherwise is to die in spirit as well as flesh.

Once more I weep, bowed under the heavy load. Give me the strength to stand straight and walk proudly. Give me companions to share the weight. But no one comes. My companions, too, are bowed low. They do what they can, but it is not enough and they call to me for help. Why, oh why, hast thou forsaken me? And, still no relief.

Then slowly the dawning comes, as I take one faltering step at a time. I creep steadily up the hill. Others have been here before. I follow their trail of sweat, tears, and blood: I can see the way. With each wavering step I gain in confidence. My strength is fed by my own resolve. Here is my purpose. Here is my meaning: To live the life which is handed to me with courage. To carry my burdens with dignity. To focus the strength which is my inner being rather than squander my resources on outward despair.

I am renewed! I find new life in my courage to be what I must be. It is my resolve that is reborn and I open my eyes as a baby for the first time. There, around me and beside me, are others carrying their burdens. We nod encouragement to one another.

I give them thanks for this resurrection. Amen.

– Sydney Wilde

For Easter Day or Other Times

O God we thank thee for the stir of thy Spirit within us;
for the courage which is equal to every new day;
for the hopes which rise out of the failures of yesterday;
for the resolve which lifts its head above wrong and woe,
and affirms its right to repent and begin again;
for the life which cannot be holden by death;
for the healing which comes to wounded hearts through time;
for the sunrise which is greater than our fires and ashes;
for the joy which breaks in we know not how and when
least expected;
for the disappointment which releases better desire;
for the darkness where the roots grow;
for the golden thread of valor and goodwill never lost
through all the strange wanderings of man.
for all the labors of those who have sown that others may reap;
for the high calls to duty in our day and time;
for the goodness which is at the heart of the world;
for the spirit of Jesus Christ;
for all the saints;
for all we love;
for the longing of this our prayer. Amen.

– Vivian T. Pomeroy

An Easter Prayer

As the earth, O God, is resurrected into life, and we see once more its beauty, so may it be with our souls. Let the winter-time of doubt dissolve and all the frozenness of our refusals melt within us. Deepen our faith that evil shall be vanquished, that good at last shall be triumphant. Let no Easter come to earth, O God, and come not to our spirits! Revive our faith! Let the sepulchers of our despair be opened! Let darkness pass; let dread be left behind! Let weeping be turned into joy, and lamentation into singing! And the beauty of Thy peace, O God, let it be upon us. Amen.

– A. Powell Davies

God, I search for you at Easter.
Where do I look?
I will seek you at Golgotha,
And find a man dying in despair.

We killed him, we still do.
This man frightened us, you see.
He offered us freedom, but we hid in our cells.
He gave us love, but we shut it out.

But he wouldn't give up, he still won't.
He found us in our pride
       in our hypocrisy
       in our deceit
       in our cruelty.
Our life, he said, was death.

Maybe there's something in him though, we thought;
Jesus can be our Messiah
       our King
       our Superstar
       our God,
But he pricked the bubble of our idolatry.

And so in ignorance and frustration we turned on him.
He lived in Palestine, we killed him there.
He lives in us, we kill him there, too,

The prisoners slaying their deliverer.

But they say he's alive again!
Through humiliation, pain, and death—to life!
Life freed from fear, from greed, from hate.
True life is liberty in love.

Christ offers us life, liberty, love,
And these, God, are yours to give.
There on the Cross on Good Friday,
There in the garden, God, on Easter Day,
I've found you.

– Cliff Reed

Prayer for Life and Death

O Thou who art the Lord of Earth and Sky, of Life and Death, we thank Thee for thine infinite wisdom which hath created so marvelous a world, and evolved us to be exercised with it. Thou hast made challenge our teacher and growth our guide, hope our spur and happiness Thy harbinger. Thou hast made love Thy creative force and death Thy servant in clearing away that which can no longer hope and grow and love and create.

We pray for the grace to see life and death in their proper perspective, and as we praise Thee for life, with its challenge, learn to give Thee thanks for death also with its change and the rest and peace which come at the last. We would become more aware of its dark and solemn beauty, of the past years it hides, and of the new birth it heralds in the realm of the spirit where all good that has been unites in the growing light of God.

As we give ourselves to life, help us also to make our peace with death, and let us, when it must come, make it welcome, but before then, bid it bide its time. Let hope be our banner, mercy be our guide, each in its proper place, our song of joy.

– Donald S. Harrington

Easter

O God, who art spirit, help us to speak to thee now in the language of the spirit. Put us for these few moments of prayer out of touch with earthly vanities, and more in accord with the things of heaven. Open our eyes to discern the frailty of that which is seen, and the permanence of that which cannot be seen. Let love and truth and honor be more precious to us this day than earthly fame and success. Let hope shine more brightly, and courage and trust be strengthened.

Those of us who come before thee with deep questions to ask, and deep longings to be satisfied, do not thou send empty away, but in mercy, comfort and bless. Let thy day bring into their hearts its light and beauty and speak its comfortable promise. Let it turn their ashes to beauty, their mantles of heaviness to garments of praise. Bless all forlorn and forsaken ones; all broken hearts and empty lives; all who are dead to honor and dead to hope. Let the miracle of rebirth which we see in all Nature about us, take place in their hearts, to touch with new life the cold fires of youth and pride and high resolve; and to reawaken in their despairing spirits the lost image of Christ.

Accept our gratitude for all this day speaks to us and brings to us. May it revive in us the tender grace of the past; the love and care by which we were once surrounded; the hope and confidence which were once centered upon us. Let it tell us that these treasures are still ours, undiminished by time, uninjured by separation.

May the day find us ready for these holy messages, quick to hear, eager to learn, prompt to obey. And may it leave us blest and cleansed, our doubts quieted, our fears allayed, our path of duty made straight and open, our spirits jubilant and our feet swift to tread those paths, and find our journey's end in the welcome of thy love. We ask in the spirit of our Christ. Amen.

– Charles Edward Park

Easter

We thank Thee, O God, for all the stirring of life renewed, for the warm winds and the whispering of leaves on trees, for the sweet new fragrance, for the brave colors of life's streaming banners, carried once more to victory over death. And for the soul's triumph, and the transmuting of tragedy, and for the true and the good which are crucified but never die. Breathe into us, O God, the quickening breath of the life which was before the pageant of the world began and shall be evermore. Amen.

– A. Powell Davies

Rolling Away the Stone

In the tomb of the soul, we carry secret yearnings, pains, frustrations, loneliness, fears, regrets, worries.

In the tomb of the soul, we take refuge from the world and its heaviness.

In the tomb of the soul, we wrap ourselves in the security of darkness.

Sometimes this is a comfort. Sometimes it is an escape.

Sometimes it prepares us for experience. Sometimes it insulates us from life.

Sometimes this tomb-life gives us time to feel the pain of the world and reach out to heal others. Sometimes it numbs us and locks us up with our own concerns.

In this season where light and dark balance the day, we seek balance for ourselves.

Grateful for the darkness that has nourished us, we push away the stone and invite the light to awaken us to the possibilities within us and among us—possibilities for new life in ourselves and in our world.

Amen.

– Sarah York

Spring

Spring Housecleaning of the Spirit

Julian Huxley, the great humanist, once wrote: "It is of the greatest importance that humanity now and then should take out its beliefs for spring cleaning." Perhaps the same is also true of the human spirit.

In the holy quiet of this promising hour of spring,

May we purge ourselves of coldness of spirit that warm spring breezes may thaw our souls;

May the debris of wrongs unforgiven be gathered and discarded so we can start anew;

May slowness of spirit, frozen by cold, be quickened to every fresh possibility;

May the song that has lingered too long in our lungs be inspired by twittering bird choruses;

May the grime of mistakes made be rinsed from our minds with the springtime waters of self-forgiveness;

May the dust of the exhausting journey be wiped from the furniture of our lives so that it gleams again;

May we muster the strength to do our own spring housecleaning of the spirit.

– Richard S. Gilbert

The Spring

O God of life, who dost renew the face of the earth and dost quicken all things, we bless thee for this lovely time; we praise thee for all beauty it brings to our eyes and for all the cheer it gives to our hearts. Forbid that we be sullen when the trees break forth into singing; forbid that we be unmoved when the great tide is flowing again. Make us eager not only to be good but also to be happier, knowing that joy is one of the fruits of the spirit. May we not defraud ourselves of the fleeting day, but drink here and now of the sweetness of life. Amen.

– Vivian T. Pomeroy

We are waiting for the sun to show its strength. The winter is too long, and spring seems to trifle with us. The everyday cold has made us tired, our neighbors and children and co-workers tired. We are waiting to rise from the dead.

Who is not ready for the poetry of spring, the forsythia that blooms overnight, the digging, the surprise of lengthening days?

May we savor the air as it grows warmer and easier to breathe. May we love the earth again, and while we wait once more for the sun to show its strength, may we care for one another.

– Jane Ranney Rzepka

A grace appears in the world on days such as these when the sun gently warms the breeze and when the sun warms the heart to simple beauty in an unfolding Spring.

Hurried feet or harried minds are apt to find a slightly less hurried pace; we may even stroll rather than race.

The city, so often cold or gray or cruel, becomes brighter; the possibilities, the promises, the hopes which fill us may return to us with new strength.

A grace appears in the world on a morning such as this when together we gather—when we gently warm this place by our presence, when the simple beauty of being human unfolds like the growing Spring.

Hurried feet or harried minds are apt to find here a gentler place, where joys are shared, sadness too, where we may meet together as comfort and hope to one another.

Life in the city sometimes cold, gray or cruel; in a church such as this - Life recalls to itself the brighter light and hope which each sacred individual possesses.

Here the possibilities, the promise, the hopes which fill us may return to us with new strength.

> So, for this day and for the night too,
> for all the gifts of Life, we gather and we
> give thanks at this hour. Amen.

— Bruce Southworth

Prayer

We have come today, as we have come to many places in our lives, in the hope of renewal.

We see around us the faint renewal of Nature:
> the streaks of green in the grass,
> the buds growing on bushes and trees,
> the sun slowly climbing higher in the sky.

And within us, we feel the urgings for our own renewals,
> a joy which joins us with the joy of the countryside
> once again blooming with Life.

Let this be our comfort and inspiration:
> that Life continually renews itself,
> and that we are able to join in It
> with our own wonder-filled growing.

Now is a time when we would pray to the Spirit of Life,
> when we would revere It as holy and sacred,
> when we would hope for It to be in every human being,
> that our earth may be a place of peace.

We give thanks for our daily food,
for that of the earth which, through its death,
continually renews us.

We remember our failings,
> and reach for the strength to forgive ourselves for them,
> as we would forgive those who have in some way
> been unkind to us—short of temper and sharp of tongue.

We would hope not to be fooled by some illusion of Life,
> and tricked into denying what is truly Real;
> yet should we thus fall,

we pray for the inner strength and the love of others
to help us back on our feet again.

Now is the time when we would clearly see the wonder of Life,
its power and glory,
and that even though things die,
Life itself is eternal and everlasting.

May we know that we touch something like immortality
when we know this with our heart of hearts.

Let us continue now with our private thoughts and prayers
in silence . . . . . .

May the life which is in us and among us
fill us to overflowing,
so that we may be fully human
and know that which is fully Divine.

In the Spirit of Love we pray,
amen.

– Daniel E. Budd

Spring

Spring is a time of movement and unrest.
It is, a poet has written, 'the cruellest time.'
It was the time of the crucifixion.
Keep our hearts steady through its storms,
Our faces firm against the rain and hail.

It is a time for pruning and for repair,
For discarding what is broken and useless,
For repairing what is worn, but useful,
May we have the judgement to know which is which,
And the strength to do what is needed with both.

Spring is a time of light and glory,
Of the snowdrop, the crocus, and the daffodil.
Open our eyes to see its gifts.
May the green gold of spring shine in our hearts,
Our spirits be filled with its coinage of beauty.

It is a time of birth and rebirth.

It is the time of Easter.
Let Easter be born in us.
> And live in us,
> And gain new being from our lives.

Spring is a time of cleansing airs.
Let us open our windows to the breath of heaven,
Our hearts to the wind of Pentecost.
> Fill our lungs with new life,
> Our sails with the breath of power,
> That we may live and sail to the glory of God.

– John Knopf

O Mystery

O Mystery beyond my understanding,
Voice in my heart answering to the earth,
And light of distant stars!

O Wonder of the spring, leading the seasons on:
The dewdrops sparkling on the web at sunrise,
And unseen life, moving in depths and shallows of the brook,
Trembling in raindrops at the edge of eaves,
Whisper to me of secrets I would know.

O Power that flows through me and all that is,
Light of stars, pulsating in the atoms in my heart.
Whether you are mind and spirit
Or energy transcending human thought
I cannot know and yet I feel
That out of pain and sorrow and the toil
Through which creation springs from human hands
A force works toward the victory of life, even through the stars.

Here on the earth winter yields slowly, strikes again, and hard,
And lovely buds, advance guards of the spring suffer harsh death,
And pity moves the heart.
Yet life keeps pulsing on
The stars still shine, the sun rises again,

New buds burst forth, and life still presses on.

O Mystery!
I lift my eyes in wonder and in awe!

– Robert Terry Weston

Let us lie back for a few moments and feel the life moving through our bodies.
With each breath, life is pulsing through us. Life: energy, movement, connection.
Let us feel the spirit of life moving through our selves.
We are not isolated, we are alive with every green and every moving thing.
Life vibrates within us, and here, together, we amplify the spirit of life.
Let us feel together how alive we are. Spring lives within us every day, sometimes asleep, sometimes awakening, sometimes vibrant with life.
Spring: the awakening of life happens not just in the world, but in us, for we are of the world, and of the seasons.
Now is the time for awakening life. Though snows still threaten, their time is past. Let us awaken to life, to wholeness, to holiness, to health.
Amen.

– Mark Mosher DeWolfe

Springtime Prayer

O God of the morning of the world, by whose bidding the earth is stirred with new life and at the sound of whose voice creation wakes and sings, open our hearts to the gladness of this season and may the freshness of its beauty cleanse our souls.

Forgive us, O God, that so dim-sightedly we go our way, in haste and fever and with fretful aims. Lift up our eyes! Let us see the wonder all about us! Not a fragile petal on the tiniest of blooms but Thou hast given it creation's glory; Thy miracle of life is wrought anew with every blade of grass.

We thank Thee, O Creation's Lord, for this renewal of life's unfolding, this revelation of Thyself that never grows old. May the joy of it restore our hope, its loveliness enrich our understanding. May the beauty of it breathe itself into our spirits, and its promise mingle with our prayers. Amen.

– A. Powell Davies

Spring Meditation

The earth does not argue. It does not debate. It acts and reacts in accord with the laws of its own being and existence. We are children of the earth and our life is one with it. We rise and we fall as we meet or refuse to meet its rules of existence.

The earth is coming green again this year and for that we are thankful. The hyacinths are in bloom and the first tulips. By them we are reminded of the morning of the world. They speak without words, but with color and form of the infinite power of sun and rain, of winter snow and summer heat. They speak without words to shame the drabness of our streets, to tell by contrast the grayness of our lives.

For the power in life that moves, ever moving, we give our thanks; for the fruitfulness of the earth and the beauty of the hills and woodlands, for wide and clean rivers, for deep lakes, for the skies and the ocean. But more than these, may we find reason to give thanks for the beauty of human life that we can make to shine; for the purity of the human soul that rests in our power to achieve; for the warmth of human love that is ours to generate.

To each of us much is given and from each of us much is expected. Let us rise to that expectation and, as silently as the sun, as the hyacinth, as the tulip, speak of the quality of human life through the day and through the year of our own living.

– John W. Brigham

Holy Spirit, cleanse our eyes that we may see the springtime glory round about us. Remove from our hearts all that has clouded them so that no longer they can see. Transform us into those that greatly endure; those that eternally trust; those that are strong in the power that comes from strength unseen. In thy Spirit may our spirits be reborn and take courage yet once more. Amen.

– William Lawrence Sullivan

VII. Fields are Smiling in the Sun

Fields are smiling in the sun,
Loosened streamlets seaward run,
Tender blade and leaf appear,
'Tis the springtide of the year.

– Frederick Lucian Hosmer

Easter Letters

It is an old custom to send out an Easter letter to the congregation, with a holiday message from the minister. Sometimes such letters enclose a schedule of Easter activities and/or an Easter offering envelope. We include here a sample of such letters from three ministers. They are also suitable as a reading during a service.

April 1985

Dear Friends:

This time of year it is popular to explain away Easter as a celebration of bursting buds and blooming blossoms. It's okay to rejoice in the greening of the earth. I rejoice, too. I'm glad that the sand and salt on the streets are now being swept away, and the sound of the peepers is sweet to the ears.

But Spring is not Easter. Easter is something else. For Spring is automatic. It always comes. Easter is not automatic. For some folks, Easter never comes at all.

If we read it right, Easter is hard work. And, if you've ever been around a barnyard or in a birthing room of any sort, you will understand. It is hard work, bringing forth life from the tomb.

Easter means much more than dancing with the daisies, and we liberals ought to pay more attention to the holiday than we do. For it affirms all of life's forces which struggle against death.

Easter says that the life of one person can be imprinted on centuries. Easter says we are tied with life struggles, millions of years gone, and to infinite years beyond. Easter calls us to stretch our lives, to reach beyond our petty concerns to large and grand dreams—as Jesus did—and at least to make some mark on those who will follow us.

In other words, Easter calls us to some measure of immortality. It need not be grand. But, by God, we can strive to respond to the call. Easter comes tough. So it brings a blessing. And, if you are touched by the blessing, all around will rejoice.

Faithfully yours,

Bruce M. Clary

The First Parish Universalist Church, Stoughton, MA

March 27, 1980

Dear Friends:

I like to think of the Spring-Easter season bursting on us in a surge of light and color and warmth—later sunsets; pale green willow, golden crocus, and the hot sun at noonday—a symphony that relaxes and revives at the same time.

It doesn't happen that way at all. It never has; but this year perhaps demonstrated it more clearly. The seasons change with many false starts and setbacks. My snowdrops hopefully poked tentative shoots above ground over a month ago. They were discouraged by a change that brought winds and rockhard ground. They tried again and were buried in snow and drowned in icy rain.

Perhaps they should not respond to the fickle warmth this morning, but they will. Snowdrops, we assume, are mindless—as are maple trees and pussy willows, but they respond in a healthy fashion to the inhospitable and the daunting.

With our complex personalities and intellect we find a great deal to doubt and stumble over. We recoil from coldness of spirit and discouragement as we try to grow. We are sensitive to our lack of success. I look on those intrepid snowdrops and wonder, "Don't you ever give up?" It's not the steady bleakness of winter so much as the encouragement given and then withdrawn. We humans speak of momentum. The hardest thing is to get going, to be thwarted and then to try again and again.

The lessons of spring are as demanding as the harsher lessons of winter. To have "spring in our souls" truly, is to have expectation and trust **combined with** resolute courage and constancy. These are priceless qualities in our personal lives and valuable in our church and our nation. If spring can teach us these lessons it will be a gift greater than the light and color and warmth.

The Blessings of the Season to you.

Janet H. Bowering

Thr Universalist Unitarian Church of Haverhill, MA

Easter 1984

Dear Friends:

We have a need to celebrate now! Open the windows of your homes and of your minds. Stand and drink in the golden sunlight. The promise is fulfilled, spring has come again.

Nearly all our religious holidays are grounded in some form of seasonal change. This is understandable since the early church wisely combined them with older agrarian festivals. And early peoples, at least in temperate climates, noted the transitions of the turning year as a crucial part of their survival in an often inhospitable land.

In a society of frozen dinners and centrally heated houses the changing seasons more often represent a change in outlook. There is a psychological shift as we move from casual summer habits to the routine of fall schedules and responsibilities.

In the same way, the tilt of our hemisphere toward the sun revives not only the vegetation, it has a heartening effect on old plans and on nascent ideas. Lives are changed by new directions and fresh possibilities.

That which the old cults displayed in the changing of the Gods, and which Christianity dramatized in the legend of a risen savior, is with us still. Whether we buy a bunch of daffodils, look for a new way to tackle a job that has gone stale, or simply gaze with awe at a young child, we are renewing ourselves.

We draw on that perennial source of life and hope presented by the returning sun—and if we name what happens to us resurrection, we will not be far off the mark.

The blessings of this season be yours

Janet H. Bowering

The Universalist Unitarian Church of Haverhill, MA

April 11, 1982

Dear Friends:

Easter is a celebration of the rebirth and renewal of life in the spring. New England winters are long and the arrival of spring is most welcome. Life is a miracle. No materialistic theory completely explains the presence of lingering snowflakes, the green grass, the yellows of dandelions and forsythia, the migratory flights of Canada geese, or the bold advent of the first robin. Neither can we explain star-filled skies or the mayflowers that grow in abundance on the south side of mountains. Existence has and always will be surrounded by mystery.

Easter is the celebration of the uncommon beauty of the commonplace world that we far too often take for granted. It also is the celebration of the courage that triumphs over tragedy, the courage manifest in living, growing things, the courage that makes human love a possibility, and the search for excellence imperative.

On Easter we celebrate the life and influence of Jesus of Nazareth. Although despised, rejected, and crucified, his invincible spirit could not be imprisoned in a tomb. His spirit has shaped our art, music, and the culture of western civilization. Countless people through the centuries have found strength in his example of sacrificial love. Our world does not need a new revelation, but a more faithful keeping of the commandment of love to God and humankind. The real enemy of the spirit of Jesus is not the doubt of Thomas but those who have no other vision beyond the exercise of power.

Above all else, Easter is the great affirmation that might does not make right —that truth crushed to the earth will rise triumphant.

Faithfully yours,

Stephen Davies Howard

All Souls Church, Greenfield, MA

Easter 1995

Dear Friends,

Once again comes the holiday which we observe in so many ways, from services for devout worship to lighthearted pleasure in a gathering of family and friends. Most of us come somewhere between in our reasons to celebrate:

Winter is past and the greening time comes, pussy willows, snowdrops and the crocus appear on the earth,

The natural world proclaims a time of new beginnings.

Days are longer, brighter, warmer.

We have come through dark and difficult times and the message is to look forward.

The legend of ancient gods and goddesses renewed and returned to vitality speak to our own hopes.

The saga of people fleeing bondage and oppression reminds us of human courage and the will to be free.

The story of a young teacher and prophet who dared to preach his message even unto death stirs us and heartens us.

If we can respond to any or all of these, we honor the good earth, the pattern and shape of creation and the striving of people through the ages.

Easter offers us another round of opportunity. It proclaims the good news that even in a worn and cynical world there is still much to be saved and treasured.

May the season warm you with life and hope.

Sincerely,

Janet H. Bowering

The Universalist Unitarian Church of Haverhill, MA

VIII. In Greening Lands Begins the Song

In greening lands begins the song
 which deep in human hearts is strong.
In cheerful strains your voices raise
 to fill the whole spring world with praise.

– Anonymous

Easter Eggs

Easter eggs have a very long ancestry—though chocolate or plastic or cardboard ones only go back a short time—but the giving of real eggs, colored or dyed, also were part of pre-Christian spring celebrations—eggs were regarded as symbols of continuing life and resurrection—the ancient Persians, Greeks, Chinese all exchanged them, at their spring celebrations.

During the fast of Lent eggs were forbidden food—so they were joyfully eaten on Easter and given as presents.

Since eggs are especially plentiful in the spring, there was a natural association with both the spring celebrations and by extension to Easter. All sorts of eggs were used, not just chicken eggs. Among other popular eggs were duck eggs, goose eggs, quail eggs, and pheasant eggs.

The custom of coloring and decorating these eggs is very old, too. Designs can be bright and colorful. Red-dyed eggs were very common in many countries. Children delight in coloring them or putting designs on eggs. Store-bought dyes are commonly used today, but if you want to use natural dyes for your eggs, you might try the following: steeped tea leaves will give various colors from ecru to dark brown depending on the strength of the tea; yellow onion skins will yield yellow or peach; red onion skins will give you red; raspberries will give you dark red; blackberries will give you a bluish tint; spinach will give you yellow green; dandelion roots a light purple.

In the Ukraine elaborate designs are painted on eggs and they are treasured and handed down within the family for generations. In many American families today a game is played at breakfast on Easter Sunday to see how many eggs belonging to others you can break before your own is broken. It is best to do this with hard-boiled eggs. This custom goes back hundreds of years—the belief was that eggs had to be broken to let the blessings out. When that happened, the believer said "Christ is risen."

In Scotland, children rolled eggs down a hill on Easter morning, said to be symbolic of rolling away the stone from the tomb where Jesus's body had been laid. Nowadays in the United States we have egg rolling on Easter morning at the White House in Washington. It is said that this custom was started by First Lady Dolly Madison. It is also a common community event to have youngsters hunt for Easter eggs (usually plastic) which are hidden in the grass at churches and other places. It is popularly said that the Easter bunny lays these eggs.

Some churches have an Easter tree. People bring decorated eggs and hang them on the tree. At the end of the service people take a different egg home with them, similar to the flower communion we celebrate in many of our congregations.

Of course, the Easter Hare is the true Easter beast. It was once considered sacred to the European spring-goddess. Instead of the "man in the moon," ancient Egyptians saw a rabbit image there. The hare is a living emblem of fertility, renewal, and return of spring.

IX. Lo, the Earth Awakes Again

Lo, the earth awakes again—
From the winter's bond and pain.
Bring we leaf and flower and spray—
To adorn this happy day.

Samuel Longfellow

Special Services

Easter Service

"He is Risen, She is Risen"

First given in the Main Line Unitarian Church, Devon, PA, 1998.

(Performance note: In order to keep the service dynamic, the readers wore lapel microphones and were able to move to different positions in the sanctuary for different sections of the service.

I suggest that you consider this service a narrative/storytelling/theatrical sort of piece, and plan to "direct" it in accordance with its dramatic structure, honoring the need for transitional pauses and moments between and during sections of the service. It runs a bit less than an hour.)

Prelude: Suggested: Handel violin piece

Announcements: *(Pacing is very important to this service. After announcements {if you must have them at all} it would be a good idea to ring a small bell or pause in some way to allow the congregation to shift moods to "sacred time.")*

Opening Words/Welcome: by Polly Leland-Mayer

"Today we come, as people have come for thousands of years, to worship and sing praises, to celebrate the victory of hope over despair, to be reminded of the ever-renewing life of the spirit, and to mark the season of springtime come again. Welcome to our festival of joy!"

Welcome to you all.

We need stories of resurrection.

We come out of the season of cold rain and darkness—blinking against the bright sun we emerge and stretch, and marvel at the bright blooms that emerge from branches once dead, from earth so recently frozen. Death and rebirth, death and rebirth—the birds sing it, the daffodils wave it, children skip and squeal and play it in the yards and the neighborhoods. It must be so—we see evidence everywhere. And so we join tonight to let our hearts and souls receive and make use of what our eyes can see: Life is Risen. Life is Risen, indeed.

Chalice Lighting and Candle Lighting:

Reader #1 (Reader #2 lights the candles):

We light our chalice as a symbol of the unquenchable light of the human spirit. May this flame be a symbol of hope in all times of darkness.

Candle #1: We light a candle in honor of Passover, the Jewish festival of freedom and redemption.

Candle #2: We light a candle in honor of the Christian holiday of Easter, to celebrate the courage and goodness of Jesus of Nazareth.

Candle #3: We light a candle in honor of Persephone, the Greek goddess of Springtime and the cycle of life and abundance she represents.

Please join in singing hymn #266

Hymn: #266 "Now the Green Blade Riseth"

Introduction/The Divine Children: Readers #1 and #2

Reader #2: You know of him. Jeshua of Nazareth, son of Mary, son of Joseph. A Jewish boy who lived in the first century in Palestine under Roman occupation. A teacher, healer, prophet who claimed to be the messiah—and some people believed him. An innocent man, a lover of humanity and of righteousness, who was executed for his troublemaking. They say he triumphed over death to rise again.

His followers wrote stories about him fifty, sixty years after his death and reported resurrection, and in those stories he is called by the Greek name, Jesus. His followers called him *the Christ*, from the Greek words, the Anointed. One chosen of God.

His religion is known as Christianity. It has been a cultural phenomenon of inestimable influence for nearly 2000 years. It is a demanding religious path that invites its followers to work for justice, to devote themselves to a life in community, to deny the world's materialism, and to receive eternal life. Its rituals, theology and literature come not only from the Hebraic/Jewish tradition of Jesus, but also from the culture of the Greeks and Romans among whom Jesus's people lived in the ancient world.

Reader #1: Yes, you know of him. You may not know of Her.

She was the daughter of Mother Earth, Demeter the Grain Mother.
Her name—Kore—which translated, simply means "maiden."
A fresh, springtime girl goddess beloved of the ancient Greeks.
She is youth itself, but far older, far more ancient than Jesus.
Just as he was called Son of God, she was Daughter of Goddess.
The two divine children who suffered undeserved cruelty and death, and
rose again to become the resurrected figures of their respective religions.

Kore the maiden became Persephone, the Queen of the Underworld.
She was stolen away to the land of the dead by her Uncle Hades, God of
the Departed Spirits. No one knows what Persephone means.
It is so old and mysterious a name as to confound scholars and
probably derives from an ancient civilization far preceding the Greeks.

Her mystery religion was celebrated for thousands years in the
Mediterranean city of Eleusis, in Greece. The yearly celebration of her
divine regeneration was known as the Eleusinian Mysteries.

Easter and Eleusis. For a period of about three hundred overlapping years,
they were *both* celebrated in the ancient world: The risen son and the risen
daughter. Persephone's observance died out and Jesus's survived. And thus
we are gathered here today, in the Christian era, paying homage to both
these resurrection stories. The truths they have to share are timeless and
universal.

Reader #2:

The epics of Jesus and Persephone have inspired countless works of art,
literature and music. A contemporary musical called "Godspell" tells the
story of the Gospel of Matthew in rock music.

This song is from that musical, but the God-image has been changed.
Today we hear it as a hymn to Demeter, mother of Persephone.

Song: "All Good Gifts," Stephen Schwartz

The Passion Narratives:

Reader #2:

Jesus had a short ministry in Palestine. Three years, really.

Some compelling sermons and public appearances, constant exhortations of his followers to love one another, mysterious warnings about the coming of the end of the world as his followers knew it, healing lepers and casting out demons, walking on water and other miracles, teaching ethics and morality in the form of unsettling, quirky parables, and most dangerously, challenging the power structures of his day. Questioning authority. Breaking rules. Subverting hierarchy.

He was arrested on the night of the Passover seder, a Thursday.

He was tried and found guilty of insurrection, mocked and flogged and crowned with thorns, and handed over to be crucified.

The gospels of Mark and Luke report:

"Then they bought Jesus to the place called Golgotha (which means the place of the skull) and they offered him wine mixed with myrrh; but he did not take it. And they crucified him, and divided his clothes among them, casting lots to decide what each should take.

It was nine o'clock in the morning when they crucified him.

When it was noon, darkness came over the whole land until three in the afternoon. At three o'clock Jesus cried out with a loud voice . . . 'My God, my God, why have you forsaken me?'

When some of the bystanders heard it, they said, 'Listen, he is calling for Elijah.' And someone ran, filled a sponge with sour wine, put it on a stick, and gave it to him to drink, saying 'Wait, let us see whether Elijah will come to take him down!' Then Jesus gave a loud cry and breathed his last."

Reader #1:

And so the human Jesus suffered and died, innocent of any real crime: a fate typical of any person who challenges and frightens the powerful and ruthless. Times have not changed.

The Roman Empire is still in business, only in different costume and speaking different tongues.

Our goddess, Persephone, is not a real woman. Her death experience is not caused by mortal politics, but by the cosmic struggle between gods and goddesses. Her story is the story of many human girls, and tells the tragically timeless story of male violence against female victims. The poet Homer tells the tale in his hymn *To Demeter,* composed (for the most part) around the seventh-century B.C.E.:

Now I will sing of golden-haired Demeter,
the awe-inspiring goddess,
and of her trim-ankled daughter,
Persephone, who was frolicking in a grassy meadow.
She was far away from her mother.
With the deep-girdled daughters of the goddess Ocean,
the maiden was gathering flowers,
crocuses, roses and violets
irises and lovely hyacinths
growing profusely together,
with one narcissus.
This was the snare
for the innocent maiden.
She knelt in delight to pluck the astonishing bloom
when, all of a sudden, the wide-wayed earth
split open down the meadow.
Out sprang a lord
with his deathless horses.
Seizing Persephone, he caught her up in his golden chariot
despite her laments.
Her screams were shrill and she called for her father, Zeus,
but no one heard.

(The translation comes from Penelope Proddow, "Demeter and Persephone" (adap.). The last three lines were composed by me in the interest of time and simplification. For a more thorough treatment of the Homeric source, see "She is Risen: Reclaiming the Myth of Persephone as a Resurrection Narrative for Women," Victoria Weinstein, 1997.)

Still glimpsing the earth, the brilliant sky, the billowing, fish-filled sea and the rays of the sun, Persephone vainly hoped to see her beloved mother again... Demeter circled the earth for nine days, steadily, brandishing shining torches, searching for her daughter, bride of Hades, unwilling Queen of the Underworld—Place of the Dead.

Meditation: "In The Place of Death"   Victoria Weinstein

Reader #2:

Innocent, they are stolen away from the sunlit world.
Precious, they are grieved by a world that loved and needed them. Loyal
    daughter of Lady Earth, the Grain Mother.
Fierce son of Abba, Elohim, the Hebrew Father-God.
They are us—we are they:
maidens, sisters, brothers, sons, daughters, goddesses,
disciples, water-walkers, stillers of the storm,
bringers of seasons and of many gifts.
We don't want them to die, to disappear into the bowels of the earth, to
cease to exist.

And so we come with Jesus only as far as the Garden of Gethsemane where
he prayed before his trial, and where he asked his disciples to keep him
company. His disciples fell asleep. Too weary, too drunk, too cowardly to
stay awake with the frightened man. "Take this cup from me," he had prayed

... And we come with Persephone only as far as the field of Nysa,
where she gathered flowers before her abduction.
Her friends, lovely nymphs, failed to save her from
the greedy clutches of Hades—Too slow, perhaps, or too distracted by the
    pretty blossoms.

We bow our heads because her mother couldn't save her.
We bow our heads because he felt abandoned by his "father."
We are as weak as the disciples, as distracted as the girlish friends.

We arrive at this most painful moments in these epics
and avert our eyes at the cross, the rape.
We cannot go with these children into Death and
their time of captivity in darkness.
It is for them to experience. It is for them to conquer.

In the silence, and in the music, we pray for patience.
We meditate on helplessness that is not permanent, not eternal.
We accompany the Son and the Daughter of Life in their time of trial.
And we bear aloft torches in the darkness, to search
and to show that we will not abandon them, or each other.

(Dim lights in sanctuary. One minute of silence)

Prayer Response: Organ solo: Bach, *Nun komm' der Heiden Heiland*

The Resurrection Narratives: *(bring lights up slowly)*

Reader #2:

And very early on the first day of the week, when the sun had risen, they went to the tomb. They found the stone rolled away from the tomb, but when they went in, they did not find the body. While they were perplexed about this, suddenly two angels stood beside them. The women were terrified and bowed their faces to the ground, but the angels said to them, "Why do you look for the living among the dead? He is not here, but has risen."

Reader #1:

After a most shocking and frightful year, when Demeter's wrath kept the earth from yielding a single seed and the race of humans was about to die out altogether from hunger, the gods relented to Demeter's rage and justice-seeking, and Persephone was released from the land of the dead. Mother and daughter clasped each other close in passionate reunion.

But because she had eaten of the pomegranate, fruit of the Underworld, Persephone was committed to returning to Hades for a portion of the year, free to spend one third of the year in the sunlit world.

She became the most dread and beloved Queen of the Underworld, gracious on her throne, greeter of departed souls, absolute sovereign of her new realm. Greek religion confirms her status as even higher than her abductor-turned-husband, the Lord Hades.

In all reports of the Eleusinian mysteries, we read of a torchlight search for Persephone. Demeter goes in search of her daughter and joyfully proclaims, "She is risen!"

Reader #2:

In the Greek Orthodox church there is a practice unique to the Greek Christian observance, and probably has Greek rather than Christian origins. On Easter Sunday morning, a priest ignites many torches while speaking the words, "He is risen!"

Celebration of Communion: Dona Nobis Pacem ("Grant Us Peace")
(I borrowed phrases from various sources out of "The Communion Book" edited by Carl Seaburg.)

Reader #1:

After Persephone's release from Hades, the poet Homer tells us that Mother Demeter once again made the earth yield grain, and revealed the secrets of agriculture to humankind, so that we might have bread, and sustenance, and abundant life.

Reader #2:

At the Last Supper with his disciples, on the eve of Passover, Jesus "took a loaf of bread, and after blessing it he broke it, gave it to them and said, 'Take; this is my body.' Then he took a cup, and after giving thanks he gave it to them, and all of them drank from it. He said to them, 'This is my blood of the covenant, which is poured out for many.'"

Reader #1:

In her period of mourning for her absent daughter, Demeter took on the guise of a elderly woman and went to travel among the mortals.

During this time, one of her companions attempted to cheer the sad mother by offering her a cup of red wine. Demeter refused. It was not right, she said, to drink red wine. She told the woman to make her a drink of barley-meal and water, a humbler concoction.

(This episode appears in the Homeric source, lines 206-9. It is Metaneira who offers the drink, which is refused by Demeter in favor of the barley-meal /water mixture. In the Homeric source, the brew also includes "tender pennyroyal," a hallucinogen. This brew probably refers to a special vision-inducing concoction consumed by initiates at Eleusis. However, I do not recommend providing such a beverage to your congregation. We decided on non-alcoholic beer for ours. V.A.W.)

Reading: "The Bread We Eat Is The Whole Cosmos"
from *Living Buddha, Living Christ* by Thich Nhat Hanh

Reader #1 or #2 *(while other Reader prepares the communion elements)*

"The message of Jesus during the Seder that has become known as the Last Supper was clear. His disciples had been following him. They had had the chance to look into his eyes and see him in person, but it seems they had not yet come into real contact with the marvelous reality of his being. So when Jesus broke the bread and poured the wine, he said, 'This is My body. This is My blood. Drink it, eat it, and you will have life eternal.' It was a drastic way to awaken his disciples from forgetfulness.

When we look around, we see many people in whom the Holy Spirit does not appear to dwell. They look dead, as though they were dragging around a corpse, their own body. . . . When a priest performs the [Mass], his role is to bring life to the community. The miracle happens not because he says the words correctly, but *because we eat and drink in mindfulness.* Holy Communion is a strong bell of mindfulness. We drink and eat all the time, but we usually ingest only our ideas, projects, worries, and anxiety. We do not really eat our bread or drink our beverage. If we allow ourselves life itself. Eating it deeply, we touch the sun, the clouds, the earth, and everything in the cosmos. We touch life, and we touch the Kingdom of God.

Reader #1: *[Reader #2 brings forth the bread]*

Companions are, literally, "those with whom we share bread."

We are **companions** in this free faith, and it is in this spirit that we break bread together as a sign of our community.

[Reader #2 brings forth kykeon]

The sharing of Demeter's beverage of barley-meal and water
(tonight it comes in the form of non-alcoholic beer!)
is a mark of our communion.

We share this food and drink with grateful hearts in order
to create the "miracle of mindfulness" in this most hopeful of seasons.

> *[Holding up bread]*

We are all one body, sons and daughters of the Divine.

> *[Holding up vessel of kykeon]*

We are all blood kin; our life flows from one Source.

(Readers and soloist teach "Dona Nobis Pacem" - three parts. Congregants are invited to sing any of those sections. Explain that "Dona Nobis Pacem" means "Grant us peace," and that we sing it for each other as a prayer and a blessing)

We are invited to feed one another as a way of showing our interdependency.

When the loaf comes to you, hold onto it until the person next to you has broken off a portion. Don't be shy. It is good bread—make sure you get a good chunk. When the cup comes around, dip your bread and then hold it for the companion next to you. Dona nobis pacem. Peace be with all of us.

Closing Hymn: #61 "Lo The Earth Awakes Again"

Closing Words: *(we read this antiphonally one side of the congregation to the other)*

> Out of the dusk a shadow,
> *Then, a spark.*
> Out of the cloud a silence,
> *Then, a lark.*
> Out of the heart a rapture,
> *Then, a pain.*
> Out of the dead, cold ashes,
> *Life again.*
>
> > - John Banister Tabb

Postlude

– Victoria Weinstein

An Easter Tennabrae Liturgy

LEADER: *This is essentially a service for children. Introduce tennebrae service to children and call on readers and candlelighters and extinguishers as their turn comes in the service.*

READER 1: We don't really know much about Jesus, because he lived a long, long time ago, before newspapers and books and TV. Everything we know about Jesus is from one collection of writings called the Bible. And even that was all written down a long time after Jesus lived.

READER 2: The stories we have about Jesus tell us that he was born in very humble circumstances, that his parents were poor, that his father was a carpenter. We also are told that there was a wonderful star in the sky the night Jesus was born, and that shepherds and kings came to visit the baby.

READER 3: We don't know if those stories are true or not, but we do know that they help us to imagine just how special Jesus was, and how the people around him loved him. And so, we light a candle, and call it a Christmas candle, in honor of the birth of a great man.

CANDLELIGHTER 1: lights candle.

READER 4: We don't know anything about Jesus' growing up. We assume that he learned to be a carpenter, because his father was a carpenter, and in those days, little boys almost always grew up to do what their fathers did. We do know that he learned a lot about his religion. He was Jewish. He went to Passover celebrations, learned the Jewish law, and learned what great Jewish teachers had said. He learned this all by heart, because there were no books or pencils or schools as we know them today.

READER 5: Maybe he even thought about growing up to be a rabbi, and learning even more about his religion, but he never did. Maybe he was too poor, or maybe he liked being a carpenter, or maybe he didn't like the rabbis he knew. We just don't know. This is a mysterious part of Jesus' life . . . so let's light another candle: a candle for Jesus, the man we will never know.

CANDLELIGHTER 2: lights a candle.

READER 6: One day, when Jesus was grown up, he went to hear a popular preacher, named John the Baptist. John was telling people that the end of the world was near, and that God was angry because so many things were wrong and so many people were selfish and mean. John believed that God would judge each person after they died as to whether they were good or bad. Some people liked what John had to say, but lots of people were afraid, for they realized that they hadn't always been good.

READER 7: Jesus felt drawn to John and went to be baptized by him. Being baptized can be a wonderful experience, and in that charged moment, Jesus realized that he felt so good, so free and happy, that he suddenly knew that God's love was much more important than God's anger. He decided that it was his mission to go and tell people that they did not need to be afraid of God, that God loved them. So, here's a third candle; a candle for Jesus' call to preach, teach, and comfort people.

CANDLELIGHTER 3: lights candle.

READER 8: Jesus felt very strongly about a lot of things. He believed that it is important to love God, but just as important to love our neighbors; even the neighbors whose religion is different from ours or who are doing things we don't like. Jesus taught that we should share with our neighbors, that we should be peaceful, and that we shouldn't worry so much. He was concerned about people who were sick or handicapped, and he liked people that nobody else liked. It became very clear to those around Jesus that he was a very extraordinary man, and they loved him. So, let us light another candle for Jesus the teacher, whose words still inspire us today.

CANDLELIGHTER 4: lights candle.

READER 9: So, this was Jesus. He attracted a lot of attention and a lot of love. He helped people feel good, and he helped them to be good, which is just as important. Wherever he went in his small country, people followed him around, crowds gathered, and people listened to what he had to say.

READER 10: After about a year of this, some bad things started to happen. Jesus went to Jerusalem, the biggest city in his country. Many of the people, especially the poor people, welcomed him. The Bible says that they threw down their cloaks to decorate the road and waved branches from trees, and cheered when he went by. It was a wonderful parade.

READER 11: But, not everyone was happy to see Jesus come to Jerusalem. The officials of the city were afraid. They were afraid that Jesus would start a riot, or worse, a revolution, and that they would be held responsible. People would be killed and perhaps the officials would lose their jobs. People who are afraid often do bad things, and these officials decided that they would have to somehow get rid of Jesus. It is fear that extinguishes our candle; fear which overcomes reason and justice.

CANDLE EXTINGUISHER 1: puts out candle.

READER 12: The next day, Jesus went to the temple in Jerusalem, and what he saw there made him very angry. The priests there were cheating the people, charging outrageous prices. Jesus got so angry when he saw this that he began to shout that they had turned the House of God into a Den of Thieves . . . and he ran around turning over the tables and making a big mess.

READER 13: This, in turn, made the priests very angry. They didn't like being called thieves. They didn't like a mess being made of their temple. The fact that, in their hearts, they knew it was true, made them even angrier. Now they wanted to get rid of Jesus, too. It is anger which extinguishes our second candle; anger used for good and anger used for ill.

CANDLE EXTINGUISHER 2: puts out candle.

READER 14: The officials and the priests got together and decided to do something about this troublemaker. So, they bribed one of his friends, a man named Judas, to betray Jesus. We don't know much about Judas, or why he did what he did. No doubt he had reasons which seemed good to him. People always have reasons which seem good to them for what they do. Nonetheless, it is betrayal which extinguishes the third candle; the betrayal of friendship which was precious to both people.

CANDLE EXTINGUISHER 3: puts out candle.

READER 15: The priests and officials took Jesus before the courts the next day, and after a long and complicated discussion, Jesus was convicted and sentenced to death. It was an unfair trial; there wasn't any evidence or any jury, and Jesus wasn't guilty as charged, but they sentenced him to death anyway. And so it is that injustice was the final cause of Jesus' death. Injustice is a terrible thing.

ADULT takes candle out of the church into foyer.

READER 16: You know, there are lots of people in this world who believe that force is the best way to get what they want, even what they think they deserve. We look back now and understand why the authorities felt they had to do away with Jesus. But we can also look back and see that killing Jesus didn't do any good. Jesus died, all right, but people didn't forget what he said. Jesus was dead, but his followers loved him so much that they went on teaching in his name. Jesus was dead, but the Christian religion was born. We took Jesus' candle out of the room to show that he died; now we'll bring it back in to show that, in spite of that, he is still with us.

ADULT brings candle back into church.

READER 17: Some people believe that Jesus literally came back to life after he died, but since that never happened to anyone else, Unitarian Universalists believe that this is just another way, like the star and the shepherds, of saying that this special man and his message still lives in our hearts, and still influences the way we live and think and make meaning in our world.

READER 18: We believe that Jesus lives in our hearts when we remember to help our neighbors.

CANDLELIGHTER 5: lights candle from one already lit.

READER 19: We believe that Jesus lives in our lives when we are inspired to live, and if necessary, die, for what we believe is true.

CANDLELIGHTER 6: lights candle from one already lit.

READER 20: We believe that Jesus lives in our hearts every time we try to love and understand people who are strange to us.

CANDLELIGHTER 7: lights candle from one already lit.

LEADER: You can kill people, but you can't kill the spirit. There is good in us and it wells up in response to great men and women and to great stories. The spirit that urges us on to love and serve our fellow human beings never dies.

– Christine Robinson

Spring Ceremony

Note: Prepare sacred space with candles in spring colors set in the four directions (N, E, S, W) and a fifth for Spring and each participant's soulspace, in the center of the four. Also place here a stone, fist sized or larger. The articles and the space may be smudged with cedar and sweetgrass before the ceremony.

THRESHOLD INVOCATION *(spoken from the door)*

> Eternal Earth Mother, make communion
> with the Sun rising in the perfect East,
> ardent star of winter dreams,
> of promises lain dormant in November's soil.
> Oh, Gaia, turn your eager heart to
> hallowed winds of Spring!

SPRING SONG *(smudging of participants optional at this time)*

> Sing praise for Earth's ecstatic gifts,
> of bursting bud, of tender, greening hill.
> We raise thanksgiving prayers
> in soaking silver rain,
> Sing joy for all creation,
> Sing praise for fertile Spring!

CANDLE LIGHTING *(may be done by one person or individuals for each candle)*

EAST: Welcome, fresh warmth of Sun from your southern arc to the portals of the East!

SOUTH: Welcome, soft vernal winds, tropic-born gusts of fertility.

WEST: Welcome, sweet rains, blossoming nimbus showering your glistening waters for our greening.

NORTH: Welcome, Wingeds, hurtling, flocking, soaring to new nesting grounds.

CENTER/WITHIN: Welcome, grounding energies of rootedness and growth. May our bare feet ooze in your gentle mud, our hands tingle with your loamy grace. May we carry in our hearts your message of regeneration and rebirth.

LITANY OF GRATITUDE: *(shared among participants)*

May I be witness to the minute, the humble miracles of Spring: the spider web strung with dew, the print of mouse in mud, the eruption of the egg case.

Thank you, Goddess, for woodlands enchanted with pink Spring beauties, white Bloodroot, yellow Trout Lily, lavender Hepatica.

Blessed be the rattle of woodfrogs in the ice-free pond, the jubilant song of peepers in the swale.

Oh, Universe, thank you for the splendor of the stars —Arcturus in the Eastern twilight sky, gleaming herald of Spring.

Mother Earth, may we rejoice in your fierce fecundity! Howling coyotes, hooting owls, bubbled clumps of frogs' eggs in a puddle.

Thank you, Grandfather Sky, for warm thermals rising beneath the wings of soaring hawks.

Blessed be, Oh, Gaia, for your moist, glossy, green rebirth! for Spring!

CELEBRANTS MAKE OFFERINGS TO A SPRING BUNDLE *(cotton fabric in a spring color is laid out and participants make offerings of things which mean Spring to them, e.g., pussywillow, forsythia, soil, seeds, a baseball card, shed pet fur. The bundle is smudged. It may remain open during the remainder of the ceremony/party. During the offering the participants chant either clapping or with rattles/drums)*

> We are the stars in the earth,
> We will keep her spirit pure,
> We will bring the soul rebirth!

STONE MEDITATION/CLOSING

(The stone which has been placed in the center of the candle arrangement is held and passed among the group as the leader shares the meditation.)

> For thousands of eons this stone has been witness, Witness to
countless millions of Springs in passing; Passing through melting heat and
glacial cold, Cold into warmth into swelter into ice again.
Again rebirthing into lilting grace of Spring.
> May we honor our Mother's rebirth with our witness,
> May we, as the stone, honor in stillness. Ground us as rivers flood,
furrows are turned, hills explode into green. May our hearts lift with the
growing light, sing with the rushing brook, exult with the flowering trees!
> May all Blessed Be.

(Following the ceremony/party the Spring bundle and the Stone Guardian are taken outdoors and placed together where they may mingle with the elements.)

– Ellen Dionna

X. Now Once Again the Heaven Turns

Now once again the heaven turns
To bring again the verdant year.
And once again the old sun burns
To freshen up the earth to bear

—Kenneth Patton

Story

Easter services are often intergenerational services. This story includes a candy communion of Swedish fish.

Catching Fish
by Mark W. Harris

(To tell this story you need two fishing nets; the first is empty and held up during those times in the story when the text indicates that everyone should shout: **EMPTY***. The second net is full of the candy, Swedish fish. These are given out after the net is shown to be* **FULL***.)*

The day broke cloudy. It had been only three days since those terrible events in Jerusalem. They took our master Jesus, and we barely tried to stop them. He received the ultimate sentence, and no one stood up for him. Least of all us. He is gone now. Never to brighten our hearts with his great stories and compassionate heart again. I swear he could forgive a wolf for stealing a lamb, as long as the wolf had a repentant heart. I can't believe how horrible I feel. We loved him, but we didn't have the courage to stand up for what we said we believed. The master would probably forgive us, too. I don't know how. We are such scoundrels. We deserve to be fed to the wolves for what we have done.

Now here it is early morning. There are my friends below me lying on the beach. They are trying to sleep, but it is hard when your heart is so heavy with grief. As for me, I've been awake since we fled from Jerusalem. I was afraid someone would say, "Hey there goes the son of Zebedee, wasn't he a friend of that preaching fool we arrested and hung by his heels? Good riddance to all these radicals." I just don't know what to do with myself now. What are we waiting for? What do we think is going to happen? I tried picking up some stones from the beach here at the Sea of Galilee. Normally I love to skip them across the water. But today they all seemed to sink. I went out fishing before dawn. I even took Peter along. He is supposed to be the expert, but we didn't have much luck. When the master was with us, we always seemed to pull up nets that were full, but today, it was obvious that his spirit wasn't with us. Every net we pulled up was **EMPTY.**

They say that fishing is best at dusk or just before dawn, but last evening at twilight was no good either. Three of us set off from shore just as the sun set over the hill looking toward the great open sea beyond. We had just finished mending our nets. The ropes were cracked and full of giant holes. Why Jonah's whale could have swam through. But we stitched and stitched. The holes are small enough now to hold a tiny minnow. No more excuses for not landing a good catch. We had spent all day repairing those nets. And it was pouring rain all that time. It reminded me of those days only three short years ago when my brother and I spent all our days fishing with our father. Dear father, he must curse us now for running out on him. And what have we come to? Three years of running around the countryside preaching this gospel of loving your enemy; telling those who lorded it over others that one day they would be last. Who was last now?

We feel so worthless. It reminds me of those days when Jesus first came to us. My brother and I were standing there, when the teacher came along. He said, "Join me, and we will fish for the souls of men and women. We will bring compassion to those who feel rejected, and we will scold the evil ones and tell them to repent." He was so convincing we followed him, and would have kept following him if we didn't turn out to be such cowards. Poor father, his jaw dropped as he saw us walk away. We walked out on him, and later we walked out on Jesus. No wonder the fish don't want to come near us. So there we were last night, dropping our nets time and again on the right side of the boat. Eventually it became too dark to see, and we barely made it back to shore and our campsite. What a waste. We were trawling with our nets all over that sea, but had no luck at all. Every net we pulled up was **EMPTY.**

It was late morning when we decided to go out on the water again. We were getting so hungry. What happened to all our fishing skills? It just seemed like we had lost all confidence, and couldn't do anything right. This was our prize for deserting the master—starvation. Then we saw this figure coming up the beach. Then we heard her shout out, "Have you anything to eat?" She looked vaguely familiar to us, but we couldn't quite place her. She said we had come to her home once, and visited with her and her sister Martha. We told her how sad we were, and how life would never be the same again. It's over, we said. Hopeless. We can't even catch any fish for breakfast

Every time we go out on the Sea of Galilee our nets come up **EMPTY.**

Then, believe it or not, she scolded us. It was like having the master there. She said, "What's the matter with you? Moping around like you can't do anything without him. Giving up? What would Jesus say about that? Here you are at the beach, all together, the twelve of you, now you must take care of each other. He has many followers. We are scattered now because of the fear in the city, but we will rise again. His words and stories are too wonderful to die. It's not really over. Sure, he is gone, but you have to remember what he has taught you, and then tell his stories to others. There is good news to relate throughout this whole land." She was right. If we stayed forever sad about what we hadn't done, then nothing would ever happen. We had each other. We had the memory of him as well. Suddenly we realized we could make his spirit live, and remembered how he once said, "I am with you always."

After that, we were determined to catch some fish. Our heads had been hanging so low we never would have caught anything. We needed the life, the spirit, the energy to do this, just like we always had when Jesus was with us. But he always had some special trick, some magic. We thought, what could it be? Our friend Mary suddenly snapped her fingers and said, "Of course. The master always was saying try it a new way. You can't just stay stuck on the same old thing, you have to be open to the new. Of course. Cast your nets on the left side of the boat." And so with renewed hope we sailed off from the beach with Mary watching from the shore. Soon we neared the center of the crystal blue sea, and threw our nets over the left side. In minutes we pulled them back up. We were so excited we couldn't wait any longer. We looked, and the nets were **FULL.**

What a sign. Now for a hearty breakfast of fish, cooked over the burning embers of that fire that kept us warm all night. We weren't alone on that beach anymore. We remembered we could be filled with a burning passion for life. It was like Jesus' spirit was moving among us. We were so happy with our catch we ran up to the village nearby, and said "Share our fish with us." He was gone, but his life was not. It was a great day for a celebration!

Sermons

A dilemma some Unitarian Universalist ministers face is "What shall we preach on Easter Sunday?" For your inspiration and encouragement, we present two sermons which may be helpful. One was preached by a distinguished minister of two generations ago, Vivian T. Pomeroy, at Milton, Mass. in 1942 after the death of his wife of many years. The second was preached in 1996 at Chelmsford, Mass. by Karen Lewis Foley.

Day-break
by Vivian T. Pomeroy

"Simon Peter saith unto them, I go a fishing . . . and that night they caught nothing. But when morning was now come, Jesus stood on the shore."

— St. John 21: 3,4

The story in which our text is set has a very appealing character. At the time it was written the Christian Movement had been gathering force for several generations; but there were many who were feeling that things were in a bad way. Arrogant circumstances seemed to be overpowering a simple tradition, and a sense of failure was darkening many hearts. No doubt the story was intended to be a parable for the encouragement of the struggling Christian Church in the second century. "Fishers of men" the Master had called his followers; and the Early Christians must often have felt they were on a dark and barren sea. "They caught nothing." After all, in spite of a growing organization, it was a little Church. The boat was so small and the sea was so big. But in those times of dismay they were encouraged to believe in the light while the darkness was unbroken. The morning would come; the assurance of a guiding presence; the casting of the net on the right side; and then they would not be able to draw for the multitude of fishes. "Christ turns all the sunsets into dawns," at last said one of them.

But because the story was written with spiritual insight, there lies in it the suggestion of a more intimate truth. It lives again marvelously as the story of personal experience; it strangely calls to the hearts of any of us today. So listen to it repeated in this tone.

There is the man Simon Peter. The time is immediately after the death of Jesus. Life has tumbled in on Peter. Things he thought secure have been all broken up. The worst has happened. For him the world has been despoiled. The stunning waves have gone over him. Now he returns to the scene of his former job as fisherman on the Sea of Galilee; goes back to the very place where not so long ago he had left his nets, when that irresistible voice called him: "Follow me." He goes back, not for any sentimental reasons, but simply because there is nothing else to be done. The place is the same; everything is the same, just as if nothing awful had happened. The quiet light on the water; the familiar village by the shore; the men busy with their little ships; the children at their play. The unchanged, undisturbed, indifferent scene is a dull offence to this man wholly occupied by a single grief. But the sea calls to labor. There is the old common work again. The old habit re-asserts itself. Peter says: "I go a fishing." He says it wearily. He is going back to the old prosaic life with new memories like stabbing wounds; and it means work for a while in utter darkness—such meaningless, profitless, desolate work. And then across the waters of that disheartened and commonplace duty—the breaking of the morning; the lost hope stealing back again through the mist; the remembered voice speaking: from the distance which is no distance; the undying call for devotion to the living. "Simon, do you still love me? Then take care of my sheep; feed my lambs."

It may be everyone's story. When any of us men and women have met and stumbled through some dark and immense hour, the ordinary world around us seems utterly unreal. Not necessarily a dark hour; as a matter of fact, not necessarily an hour of anguish; possibly one of fearful joy. Anyhow, up from the gloomiest valley or down from the highest mount we come, and we see nothing but our own vast empty surprise. All interest in the common things of life seems stopped for ever. Almost deliberately cruel appears the unconcerned regularity of things; incredibly stupid this continued procession of daily affairs.

The world of Nature, its moods and motions, does not change a shade or pause a moment for all that we feel. We have stood in a hushed room and watched a beautiful life withdrawing from a form dearer to us than anything else the world contains. We have put our hopes into some gallant cause only to see it smashed against the hard resistance of ignorance and wrong. We have been uplifted into some supernal light. And, after it all, the surrounding scene is untouched by our amazement and grief; unstirred by our exultation. It appears to mock us. The morning sun shines cheerfully through the windows of the house;

the rain drips with no more hint of tears than before; the hills are silent; the sea-tides rise and fall. "Ol' man River, dat ol' man River, he must know sumpin', but don't say nothin'; he just keeps rollin', he just keeps on rollin' along."

Not only Nature, but the whole world of our own Humanity is all around us with its business undelayed, its movement unabated, its laughter unquenched. Once it was reported that, when the news of the death of a notorious financial magnate reached Wall Street, something occurred which had not been known before. There was a hush for fully five minutes. Frantically busy men stopped in their tracks; there was no sound of voice or footfall; even the tape-machines ceased their ticking. Only five minutes—and then the mighty tide of human affairs flowed noisily on, accentuated by the brief pause.

For most of us there is no homage of five minutes' silence. The world's needs must be met; pleasure and greed keep up their pursuit; neighbours go on their errands and keep their engagements; the children's shouts are heard from the street; the boy flings the newspaper at our door; the postman punctually rings the bell; trade is brisk in the market; the train tolls its friendly warning; the plane roars across the sky. Everything is the same.

Then we are compelled, or then we choose, to return to the simplest duties. After hours or days tremendous with excitement and dread and love and sorrow, we go into low gear and begin to climb the old hill again. Life as a whole will not bear thinking about; so we apply ourselves to some ordinary and undeniable detail. With our bewildered hearts we find ourselves among familiar things. Empty seems the old place; senseless the old work; but the place waits, and the work has to be done. It may as well be done. Our enormous experience gives us no discharge from the ranks of the little people; no immunity from the demands of the commonplace. The sunlight may seem an unearthly glitter, and our fellowmen, even the most sympathetic, may seem only shadows; but all the same the sunlight falls, the friends pass and speak. So it is back to the routine, back to the things that remain, taking life up again, although it seems only a broken bit of life. And we say: "I go a fishing."

And never again, so we think, will the heart know peace, or joy gird us for life's endeavour. Never again, we think, will there be any sense that ordinary things are highly significant and worthwhile. Least of all could this happen amid the triviality or the monotony of the tasks to which we have returned; least of all amid the drudgery of unheroic duties. So for a time we think. But the truth is that along that plain road—and only on that road—peace comes to meet us and the imperishable essence of lost things is found again. Deep in the faithful heart are the fountains of the day; the shores of dawn are there: and there sounds the voice of tender command, bidding us live on to finish the work and to greet life with "valor undismayed and happy astonishment." Amid those most commonplace, most necessary things, where the bread is broken and the fire is kindled, we must prove the greatness of the hour through which we have passed, prove it by our Christly service to a needy world. "Simon, son of Jonas, lovest thou me?... Feed my sheep."

One might not expect to hear the accent of Galilee repeated amid the genial gossip of Alexander Woolcott; but you can hear it, if you turn to a page in that book of his, *While Rome Burns.* Here is the incident in almost all Woolcott's own words. A well-known American woman, sitting down with her stunned mother's heart in a New York hospital and staring blindly into the future, only half listening to the head nurse, who, being a wise person, kept on talking about the hardest part of her job. Had Mrs. Norris, as she waited in the ante-room, chanced to notice a shabby little boy sitting out there cooling his heels? No, Mrs. Norris hadn't. Well, there was a case, the nurse said. That boy's mother was a young Frenchwoman whom the ambulance had brought to the hospital a week before from the dingy home to which she and her child had drifted. The two had only each other in the world, and from sun-up to sun-down each day he had come and waited outside, just on the chance that he might be allowed to speak to her. Besides, he had no home where she was not. Well, that frail, valiant mother had died a half-hour before, dropping out of sight like a pebble cast into the ocean, and now it was part of the nurse's job to go out and tell that child that, at the age of eight, he was alone in the world. "I don't suppose," she suggested hesitantly— a wise woman that nurse must have been—"I don't suppose," she said, "that you would go out and tell him for me." And what happened in the scene which followed, when Mrs. Norris cleared her eyes and went forth to this new assignment, you will remember or you can imagine or read for yourselves.

"Jesus said to Simon Peter, Simon son of Jonas, lovest thou me more than the others do? He saith unto him, Yea, Lord, thou knowest that I love thee. He saith unto him, Feed my lambs."

That unchanged face of Nature, which appeared at first to mock by callous indifference our singular loss, becomes a constant invitation to a larger emotion, a more generous emotion; becomes an outward sign of a realm more safe from hurt than our weak holding. And our thoughts begin to flutter up from the little heap of mournful dust into the rays of some indescribable divine purpose of perfection, which is betokened by the sun that shines and the rain that falls alike on the sorrowful and the glad. And we come to echo the robust cry of G. K. Chesterton:

> Thank God, the stars are set beyond my power.
> If I must travail in the night of wrath;
> Thank God my tears will never vex a moth,
> Nor any curse of mine cut down a flower.
>
> Men say the sun was darkened; yet I had
> Thoughts it beat brightly on Calvary.
> And He that hung upon the torturing tree
> Heard all the crickets singing, and was glad.

"I go a fishing." That inevitable return to some active share in the world's affairs; that taking life up again among the inevitable things of every day—carries with it a wisdom greater than at the time we know, and it brings us at last to the shore of unyielding fortitude and quiet assurance. We come to be very grateful that life is largely commonplace, that it is crowded with duties, and that its unfading beauty stands very close to the most homely tasks. "I go a fishing." We all say it some time; and then we know very deeply what Charles Kingsley meant when he wrote: "Thank God when you get up that you have something to do that day which must be done, whether you like it or not."

So, as we put it, we just "carry on;" we are following on; we bend to the oars and try our best to keep time with the others—the others in the little boat, so little on the great dark waters. And then lift our eyes to the first gleam of the soul's invincible day-break.

There is only this to add. Whether we know it or not, it all has to do with the burning heart of real religion. "Now it's goodbye," says Peter in his hopeless whisper; in any age this Peter, who is no saint but a plain man. "Good-bye forever, Master. You know I really did love you still. I meant to fight loyally for your throne; only at the end I just wasn't brave and good enough. Now I'm going back to the thing I used to do." Then comes the answer: "It needn't be good-bye like that; it can't be. I haven't gone to be among the pomps or the spectres, and you didn't leave me in the place of bitter tears. I am where I told you I would be, among the living and the least of my brethren, anywhere with the suffering and the heavy-laden and the happy ones and the young children. So it can't be good-bye—not like that."

For, as Albert Schweitzer wrote and sealed with his own working faith: "He comes to us as one unknown, without a name, as of old by the lake-side he came to those men who knew him not. He speaks to us the same words—Follow thou me!—and sets us to the tasks which he has to fulfill in our time. He commands. And to those who obey him, whether they be wise or simple, he will reveal himself in the toils, the conflicts, the sufferings, which they shall pass through in his fellowship; and as all ineffable mystery they shall learn in their own experience who he is."

Born Again: Hope For Our Lives
by Karen Lewis Foley

We live by the stories that grow out of the stuff of our lives. People get to know each other by the stories they tell each other. "That happened to you? Oh, something so much like it happened to me too!" One of my own stories I call "Muskrat Revival." Years ago, just after my marriage ended and my first post-marriage romance had crashed in flames, a friend introduced me to the Great Meadows Wildlife Reservation. It was the end of March, freezing cold, with a high wind whipping the fat red buds of swamp maples in a miracle of blue sky. I was in excruciating emotional pain. My friend told me I'd get through this hard time because I was fully experiencing the loss and pain and not trying to hide from them. That seemed small consolation at the time. The best consolation was that I had a friend who would take me for a walk in such a place. And then we saw a sad sight: a dead muskrat, half frozen in the broken ice at the water's edge. The stillness and silence of the frozen muskrat seemed to echo the lack of hope I felt in myself.

After that I often walked in Great Meadows, especially when I was sad or perplexed. The friend who'd brought me there was killed in a plane crash. Sometimes I went there to be in the presence of his spirit. Three years after our first walk, I found myself there again, alone, on Easter Sunday afternoon. I'd recently ended another important relationship, and I was lonely, but the walk that day was more of a celebration. I had a new sense of purpose in my life and a goal: I was preparing for the ministry. I felt blessed by grace, by vocation, by my children and good friends, and by the memory of my dead friend, the very person who'd helped me see my vocation. The sun was again bright, the sky another brilliant blue, the trees again full of red buds, but the air blew with gentle warm breezes this Easter Sunday, and there was no ice over the water's sparkling expanse. Suddenly I heard little noises from the water—**eep eep**—and looking closely, saw several sleek dark heads coursing through the water, muskrats gleefully chasing each other, very much alive, and full of muskrat mischief. I almost laughed aloud. I wished my friend could see them, "The muskrats are alive now!" I wanted to tell him.

And so was I. He had been right, of course. Incredible blessings had arisen out of the pain of that day three years earlier. I could only think of what had happened in my life as a kind of being "born again." The most significant part of my rebirth, my finding new value and purpose in life, had involved finding a UU church, growing in faith, and developing a vocation. The Unitarian Universalist church and its people had given me a community of faith where I was free to grow my soul. And I'd heard others speak, who'd found this faith, of feeling "born again."

That is one of my stories. It probably echoes some of yours. Early Christians survived and grew in community by a common story—the story of their last meal with their teacher, of his betrayal, his trial, his execution, of the empty tomb on the third day—and of what that emptiness portended. Then added to the story were tales of his appearance in the flesh to his closest friends. **Of course** we don't know what really happened to his body. What lived for certain was the story—and perhaps the miracle of Easter is that such a story still holds such power for so many today. I imagine those early Christians felt as if they'd been "born again"—as if they'd found new faith and hope for their lives—through the experience of their story and through sharing it with each other.

In order to participate in Easter with any meaning beyond the renewal of nature, we Unitarian Universalists need to understand the Easter story within the parameters of our own faith—which holds a healthy dose of skepticism about miracles. UU minister Art Severance speaks of our need to translate:

> So for Easter, for Passover, for Spring festival, we translate old words into new understanding and meaning, archaic unbelievable beliefs into rational ways of living and loving. Some words or phrases are tricky to translate from one language into another. The advertising slogan "Come Alive with Pepsi," lost something when translated into German where it became: "Come Alive Out of the Grave with Pepsi," or as in one Slavic country: "Pepsi brings your ancestors back from the Grave." So let us rejoice in our own interpretation. Rejoice!

He is risen! She is risen! Death does not end relationship though it changes the shape and form of the one we love; while the husk may die, the seed which is planted in just one loving heart lives forever.

And so the concept of "being born again" has taken new, translated meaning for me—and it is real. It's not a pat theological formula for my future-world salvation, nor a once-for-all-time flash of mystical experience that exonerates me of all the wrong I've ever done and guarantees I'll never do it again. It's not a slogan I can carry with me and wave in people's faces to let them know I'm spiritually superior to them and if only they'd accept **my** spiritual metaphor they'd rise to my level.

Being born again just means that I've groped my way, slowly and painstakingly, to a larger faith than the uncertainty that used to sustain me, to a greater hope for my life and for the world than the bleaker view I used to entertain, and that I've learned to live with an undercurrent of joy and expectation, while engaged in the daily vicissitudes that beset us all.

And more than this, being born again doesn't stop anywhere. It keeps happening. It's a constant remembering, recommitment, re-engagement. It's not cheap grace. I find I have to keep working at it. And maybe that's the only kind of rebirth that can really speak to Unitarian Universalists—the kind we have to keep working at. It's honest. Henri Nouwen, the Dutch priest who has written and spoken so eloquently of our spiritual lives, said: "Eternal life is not some great surprise that comes at once at the end of our existence in time, it is rather, the full revelation of what we have been and have lived all along." *(The Life of the Beloved)*

Being born again is not something that some supernatural force did to me all alone; it has been, and will always be, something that happens through the vitality and the struggle of being in communion with other people. People keep birthing each other again and again. After all, my very first walk in Great Meadows was something a friend gave me in a time of pain. And I passed on the gift to another friend in a time of her own pain and confusion, when I took her there for a walk on a summer day. "Come let me show you a place that helps me get centered in my soul," I said to her as my friend had said to me. We birth each other's slow and gradual resurrections of our souls.

And finally, being born again most vividly arises out of the moments of loss and pain and bewilderment in our lives, the times when we don't know how we're going to go on, when we'd rather **not** go on, when it's all we can do to get up in the morning and put one foot in front of the other to begin our walk into the bleak and hopeless day. Who can say how it will happen for any one person in any one time of bewilderment, sorrow, anger, or despair? But going through that hard time without fleeing from our pain is what brings us to the moment—if we even recognize it—it's usually more like weeks or months—of rebirth.

Now this is the hard message. Here is the part we don't want to hear. When we come to those times of wilderness we'd rather flee, deny what we feel, and go on as if everything is the same; or we want to rush through it, find a replacement for what we've lost as quickly as possible, and we forget that it's our own feet and heart that have to carry us through. Paul Steinke, writing about how hope operates in people he's known who have AIDS, tells us this: Hope grows in the soil of despair. Unlike optimism, hope is tentative. It does not count on success or succumb to an illusion of progress… Bill came in a month before he died and told the group [of AIDS patients]: "I've been so depressed this week. I've been curled up on the couch. I've been fighting it off. It hangs on." Adrian replied: "It's all right to be depressed. When you get to the bottom, things appear differently—you see more clearly—I always feel gratified for what I have." This encouragement to inhabit despair fosters hope. ["Pastoral Notes on AIDS and Hope," *The Christian Century,* May 20-27, 1992]

John Giles, Minister of Music at the Unitarian Church of Evanston, Illinois, puts this truth in the context of making changes in our lives. It is painful to stop smoking. It is painful to face down an addict in a professional intervention. It is painful to begin family-systems therapy to address the real reason your children are acting out. It is painful to confront your parents with incest issues. When Jesus said that "in order to be born again, you must take up the cross," he was reminding us that the road to health is full of pain. ["Experiencing Our Own Resurrection," *Quest, Church of the Larger Fellowship,* April 1992]

This is where we often don't acknowledge what life teaches us again and again is true. We love Easter because of its connection with new life, because it affirms spring, because it reassures us with images of colored eggs and baby chicks and bunnies and daffodils tender and tough against the early air. But we want to get here, to Easter morning and the lilies, without enduring Golgotha. We don't want to face our personal crucifixions. The disciples ran away and pretended not to know Jesus because they didn't want to share his fate. Only the women remained, and we don't want to stand with them. We don't want to find the empty tomb and stand there in the morning light, peering into the emptiness of our lives, and wondering what it all means.

And so we rarely acknowledge Good Friday. Maybe we should. Maybe we should ritually re-enact, as peoples in every faith tradition re-enact the stories that give flesh to their spiritual realities, the pain of death that gives forth new life. Maybe we could find a way to do that in our community that would honor our multi-faceted tradition. Because the truth is, getting through Good Friday, metaphorically, is the only way to get to a meaningful Easter.

We share each Sunday morning the momentous joys and concerns of our lives. I've been aware for years that while we share certain kinds of concerns, it is extremely rare that we speak publicly of dissolving marriage or partnership, job loss, or mental illness or severe depression. It's as if we're ashamed—as if we think these hells we live through are somehow our own fault. Yet aren't these the very kinds of hell through which we need others to walk with us? I would never abrogate anyone's right to privacy. But I wonder what it would be like if those who would appreciate communal acknowledgement of their difficulty felt free to ask us to stand with them at their Golgotha,* at their empty tomb, and look with them toward their Easter?

However we die on our Golgothas, however we inhabit empty tombs, we need to hope toward our rising into renewed faith, into deeper hope for our lives, into a greater and more expansive love for those in our lives and for the world with whom we are connected. We need to keep getting born again to the truth of our lives, to the call to the best in us, to the love that sustains us and returns us ever to life. That's why we celebrate Easter not once for all time but every year. We need it every year. We need it when we rise slowly out of our deaths and despairs.

May you be born again this day, and again and again and again. And may you find here a community of companionship that keeps birthing you into new life, and discover yourself a force toward Easter sunrise for those who gather here with you.

---

* "Golgotha" is the name of the hill where Jesus was crucified: "Golgotha, the place of skulls."

XI. Spring Has Now Unwrapped the Flowers

Spring has now unwrapped the flowers,
day is fast reviving,
life in all her growing powers,
toward the light is striving.

- Piae Cantiones, 1582

Additional Resources

Lenten, Easter, and Spring Music

Composers have given us a great cornucopia of wonderful music for the Easter and Spring holiday season. For congregations planning a concert at this time of year we can only suggest some of the highlights from which they can choose. Organists, music directors, and choirs will be aware of many other delightful pieces that are available.

Samuel Barber: *Easter Chorale*
Ludwig van Beethoven: Quartet no. 15 in A Minor
Anton Bruckner: *Christus Factus Est*
William Byrd: Mass in Five Voices
Duruflé: *Ubi Caritas*
Gabriel Faure: *Palm Branches*
Orlando Gibbons: *Hosanna to the Son of David*
Hans Leo Hassler: *Herzlich Lieb Hab Ich Dich, O Herr*
Guillaume de Machaut: *Lai de la Fonteinne*
Olivier Messiaen: *La Transfiuration de Notre-Seigneur Jesus-Christ*
Wolfgang Amadeus Mozart: *Ave Verum*
Ned Rorem: *Missa Brevis*
Francis Poulenc: *Vinea Mea Electa*
       Timor et Tremor
       Tenebrae Factae Sunt
Giacomo Puccini: *Requiem*
Franz Schubert: *Lazarus* (D. 689)
Heinrich Schütz: Passion of Our Lord According to Saint Luke
Thomas Tallis: *Lamentations of Jeremiah*
Ralph Vaughn Williams: *Fantasia on a Theme by Thomas Tallis*
      Five Variations of Dives and Lazarus
Tommaso Vittoria: *Pueri Hebraeorum*
Thomas Weelkes: *Hosanna to the Son of David*

Johann Sebastian Bach: *Saint John Passion*
      Saint Matthew Passion
      Easter Oratorio

Mass in B Minor
Cantata No. 4
Cantata No. 129
Ludwig van Beethoven: *Missa Solemnis*
George Frederick Handel, *Messiah*
Arthur Honneger: *Alleluia* from *King David*
Gustav Mahler: Symphony No. 2
Flor Peters: *Trumpet Tune*
Daniel Pinkham: *Now is the Hour of Darkness Past*
Randall Thompson: *Allelulia*
Domenica Zipoli: *Festival Prelude*

Benjamin Britten: A Spring Symphony
Franz Joseph Hadyn: Spring section from *The Seasons*
Robert Schumann: 'Spring' Symphony No. 1 in B flat
Igor Stravinsky: *The Rite of Spring*
Antonio Vivaldi: Spring section from *The Four Seasons*

Easter Food

Easter Breakfast

Pancakes, which were eaten at Mardi Gras, but banned during Lent, can now be indulged in. Egg dishes predominate at Easter breakfasts, in all varieties, from scrambled eggs to eggs Florentine. Some traditions serve a pizza rustica, a special Italian egg pie with eggs, cheese, and meat fillings. And breakfast is a time for the children to crack their eggs together. We do it for fun, but originally it was an Easter greeting.

Breads include Hot Cross buns with a cross on top, to various ethnic recipes. The Polish Easter loaf is called "babka," meaning "little grandmother" because it is round and puffed out like a grandmother's skirt. It has a tree of life marked into its shiny brown crust. It is made of wheat flour, eggs, and raisins to remind us of the good things from the earth that nourish our life. There are Italian Easter breads, Irish Easter bread, Scandinavian stollen, and fruit breads. There is Russian paska, made with cottage cheese, and baked in a tall square mold, with crosses marked on each side. The Moravians make a sugar cake, called a love cake. Others make fruit cake cookies.

Pretzels have become associated with Lent and Easter for over a thousand years, and were first served in monasteries. Essentially they are bread, but like bagels are boiled in water (with baking soda added) before they are baked.

Easter Dinner

Lamb is the traditional roast for Easter dinner. It symbolizes Jesus as the "sacrificial lamb." Ham is also popular. This was ordered by William the Conqueror of England to be eaten on Easter Sunday as a proper Christian food. Lamb and ham now vie for top honors at our dinner table on Easter.

Passover

Among the traditional foods eaten at Seder meals during Passover are matzohs (unleavened breads), bitter herbs like horseradish, and roasted eggs.

Recipe

KULICH

This is a traditional Russian Easter bread. Norma Goodwin Veridan shares this recipe with us.

> 2 cups lukewarm milk
> 2 cakes yeast
> (or omit ½ cup milk and soak 2 pkgs dry yeast in ½ cup lukewarm water for 5 minutes.)
> 2 eggs, lightly beaten
> ½ cup sugar
> 2 tsps. salt
> ½ cup soft shortening
> 7 to 7½ cups all-purpose flour
> 1 cup raisins
> 1½ tsp. vanilla

1. Crumble yeast cakes into milk, or stir dry yeast and water well and add to milk.

2. Add eggs, sugar, salt and shortening to milk and yeast mixture.

3. Stir in flour in two additions using amount needed to make the dough easy to handle. When dough begins to leave the sides of bowl, turn it out onto a lightly-floured board to knead. Knead—fold dough over toward you, then press down away from you with the heel of the hand. Give dough quarter turn, repeat until it is smooth, elastic, and doesn't stick to board.

4. Place in greased bowl, turning once to bring the greased side up. Cover with damp cloth and let rise in warm draft-free spot until double in bulk. (1 ½ - 2 hours).

5. Press two fingers into dough. This will leave an indentation when dough is doubled. Punch down—thrust fist into dough, pull edges into center and turn completely over in bowl. Let it rise again until almost double in bulk. (30-45 minutes).

4. After second rising, mix into dough: raisins and vanilla.

5. Divide into 50 small buns (like hot cross buns) and place on well-greased cooking sheet. Cover and let rise until double (30-35 minutes). Bake about 15 minutes at 400 degrees.

6. To decorate Kulich: while still warm drizzle over tops Confectionary Sugar Icing, made by mixing together

½ cup sifted confectionary sugar
½ tsp warm water
½ tsp lemon juice and a bit of grated rind

Sprinkle with colored decorating candies. Serve while warm and yum!

Spring

No special food customs have developed around the celebration of Spring. People with access to lawns, garden, or the woods, however, find this a good time to add fresh growing greens to their diet. Dandelion leaves, fiddleheads, parsley, watercress, and others bring a spring flavor to the table.

Green onions, a symbol of new life to Egyptians today, are popular at this season. Moslems and Copts eat them on the day after Easter as they celebrate "sham el nessin." It is a time, they hold, for smelling the sweet breezes of spring.

Acknowledgements

The editor has made every effort to trace the ownership of material contained in this book. In the event of any question arising as to the use of any material, the editor, while expressing regret for any error unconciously made, will be pleased to make the necessary correction in future editions of this book. I want to express my thanks to the following authors, publishers, publications, and agents for permission to use the material indicated:

First, of course, to my generous colleagues whose material forms the basis of this work. They are:

Dorris Alcott
Dianne Arakawa
Mark Belletini
Janet Bowering
David Boyer
John W. Brigham
Orlanda Brugnola
Daniel E. Budd
Victor Carpenter
Gaston M. Carrier
Bruce M. Clary
Maryell Cleary
Helen Lutton Cohen
Max A. Coots
Roger Cowan
Joy Croft
Greta W. Crosby
John Cummins
Leroy Egenberger
Richard M. Fewkes
Karen Lewis Foley
Richard S. Gilbert

Philip Randall Giles
Frederick E. Gillis
Peter B. Godfrey
Donald S. Harrington
Edward W. Harris
Phillip Hewitt
Andrew Hill
Harry H. Hoehler
Earl Holt
Stephen Davies Howard
David A. Johnson
Andrew Kennedy
John Knopf
Polly Leland-Mayer
Judith G. Mannheim
Ric Masten
Colleen M. McDonald
Michael A. McGee
Judith Meyer
David J. Miller
John Hanly Morgan

Priscilla Murdock
Eugene B. Navias
Carl J. Nelson
Rudolph Nemser
Patrick O'Neill
Marjorie Rebmann
Cliff Reed
Christine Robinson
Jane Ranney Rzepka
William F. Schulz
Bruce Southworth
Betsy Spaulding
Lynn Ungar
Frank Walker
Robert R. Walsh
Victoria Weinstein
Clarke Dewey Wells
Sydney Wilde
John B. Wolf
Sarah York
Robert L. Zoerheide

I want to express my gratitude also to Ellen Dionna for permission to use her material and that of her mother Dorothy Parsons East, Freda Carnes for permission to use material by her late husband Paul N. Carnes, William DeWolfe for permission to use material by his late son Mark Mosher DeWolfe, Eva Morin, for permission to use material by her late husband Roland E. Morin, Peter Lee Scott for permission to use material by his late father Clinton Lee Scott, Marilyn Steeves for permission to use material by her late husband Addison E. Steeves, Chris Trapp, for permission to use material by his late father Jacob Trapp, Elizabeth Silliman for permission to use material by her late husband Vincent B. Silliman, and to Muriel Davies for permission to use material by her late husband, A. Powell Davies.

My thanks to the following publishers holding copyright on the selections specified for permission to reprint:

To the Ballou Channing District for "In Praise of Spring" by Dawn Goodrich from *Light Me Through: A Meditation Manual.*

To Beacon Press for the quotation from Frederick May Eliot from *Frederick May Eliot: An Anthology,* edited by Alfred Stiernotte; and for the poem by Jay William Hudson from *Prayers of Aspiration.*

To the Unitarian Universalist Association for "Prayer at Easter" by Clarke Wells, "Place of the Skull" by Leonard Mason, and "Blessing the Blend" by Jane Rzepka.

Special thanks to the following individuals for their assistance: Barbara Hutchins, Jacqui James, Eugene Widrick, John Gibbons and Joan Goodwin. Also, my deepest gratitude to Susan Weidner for her office assistance in preparing this book for publication. The publication of this book would not have been possible without the devoted support of Alan Seaburg. It is a memorial of love for his brother.

Bibliography

Findlow, Bruce. *I Question Easter.* London: The Lindsey Press, 1966.

Frazier, J.G., edited by T.H. Gaster. *The New Golden Bough.* New York: Mentor, 1964

Helfman, E.S. *Celebrating Nature: Rites and Ceremonies Around the World.* New York: The Seabury Press, 1969

Hewett, Phillip. *What Easter Means to Unitarians.* Unitarian Church of Vancouver, Britsh Columbia, Rev. ed. 1987

Hole, Christina. *Easter and Its Customs.* London: Richard Bell, 1961

Newall, Venetia. *An Egg at Easter.* Bloomington, Indiana: Indiana University Press, 1971

Purdy, Susan. *Jewish Holidays.* New York: J.B.Lippencourt, 1969

Sechrist, Elizabeth and Woolsey, Janet. *It's Time for Easter.* Philadephia: MacRae, 1961

Simon, Norma. *The Story of Passover.* New York: Harper Collins, 1995

Starr King School for the Ministry. *Easter.* Boston: Unitarian Universalist Association Department of Education, 1956

Waskow, Arthur I. *Seasons of Our Joy: A Handbook of Jewish Festivals.* New York: Summit Books, 1982

Watts, Alan. *Easter: Its Story and Meaning.* New York: Henry Schumann Inc., 1950

Weinstein, Victoria. *She is Risen: Reclaiming the Myth of Persephone as a Resurrection Narrative for Women.* Berwyn, Penn.: Persephone Project, 1997

Various bulletins over the years from the Religious Education Department of the Unitarian Universalist Association and the Church of the Larger Fellowship.

Children's books

Barth, Edna. *Lilies, Rabbits, and Painted Eggs: The Story of the Easter Symbols.* Illustrations by Ursula Arndt. New York: Houghton, Mifflin/Clarion Books, 1970.

Fisher, Aileen. *The Story of Easter.* Illustrations by Stefano Vitale. New York: Harper Collins, 1968, 1997.

Heyward, Du Bose. *The Country Bunny and the Little Gold Shoes.* Ilustrations by Marjorie Flack. New York and Boston: Houghton, Mifflin, 1939.

Zolotow, Charlotte. *When the Wind Stops.* Illustrations by Stefano Vitale. New York: Harper Collins, 1962, 1995.

Index of Authors